THE
LEBENSOHL CONVENTION
COMPLETE
IN CONTRACT BRIDGE

THE
LEBENSOHL CONVENTION
COMPLETE
IN CONTRACT BRIDGE

Ron Andersen

Published by
Devyn Press, Inc.
Louisville, Kentucky

Printed in the United States of America.

Devyn Press, Inc.
3600 Chamberlain Lane, Suite 230
Louisville, KY 40241

ISBN 0-910791-82-1

CONTENTS

PREFACE

Expert bidding has undergone a major upheaval during the past twenty years. Accuracy, especially in competitive bidding, has become so necessary on the tournament scene that we have seen the birth of hundreds of gadgets and conventions.

Among these, one of the most useful and most widely adopted by expert players is the Lebensohl convention. Its popularity is no accident. Lebensohl has virtually eliminated the all-too-frequent aggravation we once faced at the table – what to do when partner opens one notrump and right-hand opponent overcalls.*

Suppose the bidding goes

Partner	RHO	You
1 NT (15-17)	2 ♡	?

And your hand is:

♠ 6 5   ♡ 8 4 3   ◇ Q J 10 8 6 5 4   ♣ 7.

You would like to sign off in three diamonds. At my mother's afternoon bridge club the correct response is, of course, to choke out a fearful three diamond call, fold up your hand and place it squarely in the middle of the table.

However, suppose you hear the same auction when you have:

♠ K Q   ♡ 9 7   ◇ A Q J 10 9 6   ♣ Q 9 8.

You would still like to bid three diamonds, but only if it is 100% forcing. This would allow you and your partner to probe for the best contract – probably either three notrump or five diamonds, depending upon your partner's heart holding.

Clearly, you can't bid three diamonds on both hands; your partner will have no way to tell which hand you hold.

When Mr. Boehm first publicized the Lebensohl convention, this was precisely the problem he had in mind. His solution was to give responder two DIFFERENT ways to bid three diamonds – one forcing and the other signoff.

---

*According to international authority Edgar Kaplan, the true history of Lebensohl has been lost forever. Sometime in the late 60's it began to appear on convention cards, and it was thought to be the brainchild of Kenneth Lebensold (whose name had been misspelled). However, Lebensold emphatically denied any part in the convention's development. For lack of a better name, George Boehm appropriated the misspelling and introduced "lebensohl" in *The Bridge World,* (November, 1970).

It didn't take the bridge world long to realize that the principles of the Lebensohl convention could be applied to other problem areas as well.

Consider your response to partner's takeout double in the following auction:

LHO	Partner	RHO	You
2 ♠	Double	Pass	?

If you hold something like

♠ 6 3 2　♡ 9 7　◇ 10 8 3　♣ 10 7 6 5 3,

you bid three clubs and pray that partner has the good sense to stop bidding before the roof caves in.

But suppose your hand is

♠ 10 5 4　♡ K 8　◇ 10 9 4　♣ K Q 10 8 7.

You would still prefer to bid three clubs since a jump to four clubs consumes a lot of space and takes you right past what may be your only game – three notrump. This time, however, you'd be very pleased to hear partner bid again over three clubs.

Today, the Lebensohl principle is also used to handle responses to takeout doubles of weak two-bids, again providing two different bidding sequences – one to force and one to sign off.

Another problem area occurs in auctions where partner reverses:

Partner	You
1 ◇	1 ♠
2 ♡	?

If your hand is

♠ J 5 4 2　♡ 6 3　◇ Q 6 4 3　♣ Q J 5,

you would like to sign off in three diamonds.

But if your hand is something like

♠ A Q J 10　♡ 10 9 7　◇ K J 10 6　♣ A 10,

you would still like to bid a forcing three diamonds to set the trump suit so that your partnership can explore for the best game, or even slam.

Once again it is clear that you cannot bid three diamonds with both of these hands and expect partner to do the right thing.

To solve these problems, as well as other similar dilemmas, most serious players have adopted Lebensohl, a mechanism which gives responder many more options in awkward auctions where his bids would otherwise be ambiguous.

In this booklet we will examine in detail all of these applications of the Lebensohl ideas. For the sake of simplicity, we will assume that you and your partner are playing a strong notrump range (15-17 HCP). However, Lebensohl can be used equally effectively if you are playing a weak notrump.

For those readers with a taste for adventure, we'll take a brief look at some recent innovative and exciting developments in the application of Lebensohl. You and your partner may wish to try some of these new "toys" once you have become proficient with the basic Lebensohl principles.

PART I

LEBENSOHL AFTER
ONE NOTRUMP INTERFERENCE

Chapter 1

WHEN THE OPPONENTS ENTER YOUR NOTRUMP AUCTION

When an opponent overcalls after your partner has opened one notrump, you may have a difficult time bidding your hand accurately, since the enemy overcall will frequently prevent you from making your normal call.

Suppose you have something like

♠ 10 8　♡ A J 9 7　◊ 6 3 2　♣ K Q 9 6,

and hear partner open one notrump. Of course, you plan to start with Stayman and then bid three notrump or four hearts depending upon his reply. But suppose your right-hand opponent overcalls two diamonds. Now what do you do? You can no longer bid two clubs, and you certainly don't want to gamble on three notrump with three small diamonds. If you cue-bid three diamonds, the standard solution, and partner happens to rebid three spades instead of three hearts, you are still stuck with no idea where to go. Clearly you need a way to learn about partner's holdings in both hearts and diamonds.

Or perhaps your hand is

♠ 9 6 4　♡ A J 9 8 2　◊ J 10 6　♣ A 5,

and you are playing Jacoby transfers. If your right-hand opponent bids two spades over one notrump, you have lost your transfer, but you still need to find out about partner's hand, in particular about his hearts and spades.

Once the opponent's overcall has robbed you of your conventional response, you usually have to rely upon natural bidding to get you to the right contract. But even natural bids, jumps and notrump raises may become ambiguous after an enemy overcall.

Suppose your hand is

♠ 6 5　♡ 8 4 3　◊ Q J 10 8 6 5 4　♣ 7,

when your partner opens the bidding with one notrump. You will no doubt use whatever methods your partnership has agreed upon to sign off in diamonds. However, if your RHO interjects a two heart overcall you have a problem. You would still like to sign off in diamonds, but your partner may not realize that you intend your three diamond call to end the auction.

What if your hand were

♠ K Q　♡ 9 7　◇ A Q J 10 9 6　♣ Q 9 8

You'd still like to bid three diamonds, but only IF THREE DIAMONDS IS 100% FORCING. Since you have enough strength for game, you certainly don't want to sign off.

Another annoying ambiguity occurs when you have a hand where you want to raise one notrump to two or three notrump, for example:

♠ K 9 7　♡ 4 3　◇ A Q 10 7　♣ J 10 9 5

but your right-hand opponent gets in the way with a two heart overcall. It doesn't always work out well to jump to three notrump without a stopper, because partner may not have the suit stopped. If you bid three notrump and opener's hand is

♠ A Q　♡ J 5 2　◇ K 9 8 6 5　♣ A K 8

how is he to know the partnership has no heart stopper? He can't possibly guess to pull three notrump with such a normal looking notrump opener. How can either of you know that you belong in five diamonds?

Several questions arise after an overcall of partner's one notrump opening:

- Which bids are forcing?
- Which bids are non-forcing?
- Which bids are invitational?
- Which bids are natural?
- Which bids are artificial?
- How do you find out if you and your partner have a 4-4 major fit?
- What does "double" mean?
- How do you show or deny stoppers in the enemy's suit if you are interested in playing in notrump?

For the answers to these questions, most experts now use LEBENSOHL, a convention which enables a partnership to cope effectively with any overcall after their one notrump openings.

The cornerstone of the Lebensohl convention is the use of two notrump by responder as an artificial bid:

> **After an enemy overcall of partner's one notrump opening, two notrump by responder forces opener to bid three clubs so that responder can clarify his hand.**

In effect, basic Lebensohl allows responder two DIFFERENT ways to make the same bid, each with its own predetermined message for opener.

The mechanism varies, depending upon whether

(a) the enemy overcall is natural or artificial,

(b) the overcall shows one suit or two suits,

(c) the overcall is at the two-level or the three-level.

Chapter 2

LEBENSOHL AFTER NATURAL OVERCALLS

After a two-level overcall of partner's one notrump opening, responder bids as follows when using Lebensohl:

(1) A DOUBLE is for penalties.

(2) A TWO-LEVEL suit bid is to play.

(3) A THREE-LEVEL suit bid is forcing to game.

(4) A TWO NOTRUMP bid is artificial, forcing opener to bid three clubs.

Responder's rebids over three clubs:

(a) Pass with a weak hand and long clubs.

(b) Any suit bid below the rank of the overcall is a signoff.

(c) Any suit bid above the rank of the enemy suit is invitational.

In addition to the basic machinery of Lebensohl, if responder has game-going values, he has ways to

(a) ask opener if he has a four-card major,

(b) show a stopper in the enemy suit,

(c) say that he has no stopper in the enemy suit.

(5) An IMMEDIATE CUE-BID* by responder is Stayman. It promises at least one four-card major and DENIES a stopper in the enemy suit. Opener's priorities are:

(a) bid a four-card major if he has one;

(b) bid three notrump with a stopper;

(c) lacking both a stopper and a four-card major, look for a better game.

In this case opener's options are:

(1) With a minimum, opener usually bids four clubs or four diamonds. (See 3.)

(2) Opener may try a 4-3 major fit if he knows responder's four-card major,

---

*Note: Game-forcing unless the partnership fails to find a major-suit fit and also lacks a stopper in the enemy suit. In this case, responder may pass opener's rebid of four clubs or four diamonds. Therefore, with maximum strength, opener must insist on getting to game and should not rebid four clubs or four diamonds. [See (3) on next page.]

(3)With no wasted strength in the opponents' suit and a maximum, opener should jump to five of his long minor, or he should cue-bid the opponent's suit at the four-level, asking responder to pick a minor at the five-level.

(6) A DIRECT jump to three notrump over an enemy overcall DENIES a stopper in the enemy suit.
Opener then:
(a) passes with a stopper,
(b) bids a five-card major if he has one,
(c) explores for a better contract.

(7) TWO NOTRUMP followed by a cue-bid of the enemy suit after opener's forced three club call is Stayman and SHOWS a stopper in the opponents' suit. Opener must bid a four-card major if he has one, otherwise three notrump. (Since most two club overcalls are artificial, there is seldom a problem with this form of cue-bid Stayman.)

(8) TWO NOTRUMP followed by three notrump over opener's forced three club call SHOWS a stopper in the enemy suit and asks opener to pass and play in three notrump.

This machinery makes it possible to avoid three notrump when neither opener nor responder has a stopper in the opponents' suit. Yet it in no way hinders the search for major-suit fits. In addition, it clearly defines which responses are non-forcing, invitational and forcing. To gain all this accuracy after an enemy overcall, the only thing you give up is the natural meaning of two notrump by responder. Although this may seem a lot to lose, experience will soon show that you have gained heavily in the trade.

The mechanism outlined above, for showing or denying a stopper in the enemy suit, is commonly known by the acronym "FADS" — Fast Auction Denies Stopper. This refers to the underlying principle that the IMMEDIATE ("fast") cue-bid or DIRECT jump to three notrump denies a stopper in the enemy suit, while the slower auction incorporating the two notrump relay shows a stopper. Another acronym for the same mechanism is SSS — Slow Shows Stopper.

Let's go back to our problem examples and see how Lebensohl helps us handle them.

Opener	Opponent	Responder
1 NT	2 ◊	?

♠ 10 8   ♡ A J 9 7   ◊ 6 3 2   ♣ K Q 9 6

Bid 3 Diamonds. Rule 5 tells us that the immediate cue-bid of the enemy suit is game-forcing Stayman and denies a diamond stopper which is perfect for this hand. If opener has four hearts he will bid three hearts. If he has four spades he will bid three spades and you can follow with three notrump — knowing partner will not pass without a diamond stopper since you have already denied one. If opener does not have a four-card major he will bid three notrump with a diamond stopper, otherwise he will look for some other game. Whatever action opener takes over three diamonds, you can rest assured that you will reach a playable contract if you have one.

Opener	Opponent	Responder
1 NT	2 ♠	?

♠ 9 6 4   ♡ A J 9 8 2   ◊ J 10 6   ♣ A 5

Bid 3 Hearts. Rule 3 tells us that a three-level bid is forcing to game. Opener will raise hearts with three-card or better support, or bid three notrump with a spade stopper. If he has neither he will search for another game — perhaps four hearts on a 5-2 fit.

Opener	Opponent	Responder
1 NT	2 ♡	?

♠ 6 5   ♡ 8 4 3   ◊ Q J 10 8 6 5 4   ♣ 7

Bid 2 Notrump. Plan to follow with three diamonds. Rule 4 says that two notrump forces opener to rebid three clubs and that responder's subsequent three diamond call is a signoff because his suit is lower ranking than the opponents'.

Opener	Opponent	Responder
1 NT	2 ♡	?

♠ K Q   ♡ 9 7   ◊ A Q J 10 9 6   ♣ Q 9 8

Bid 3 Diamonds. Rule 3 — a three-level suit bid is forcing to game. Having created a game force, you are now free to find the right game or to investigate the possibilities of a slam.

Opener	Opponent	Responder
1 NT	2 ♡	?

♠ K 9 7   ♡ 4 3   ◊ A Q 10 7   ♣ J 10 9 5

Bid 3 Notrump. Rule 6 tells us that the direct jump to three no-trump denies a stopper in the enemy suit (FADS). Opener will not pass without a heart stopper. If he was dealt:

♠ A Q   ♡ J 5 2   ◊ K 9 8 6 5   ♣ A K 8

he will know that three notrump is the wrong contract. Following Rule 6, he can jump to five diamonds knowing he will find a fit and have good chances to make it. Responder has forced to game with nothing in hearts and, inferentially, no long suit of his own to bid.

The following deal played by Jeff Meckstroth and Eric Rodwell illustrates the advantages of the Lebensohl approach.

Vulnerable: Both
Dealer: South

North
♠ Q 10 9
♡ A J 5
◊ 7 4 2
♣ K Q 6 4

West
♠ J 8 4
♡ 6
◊ A Q 9 8 6 5
♣ 7 3 2

East
♠ 7 6 3 2
♡ Q 9 7 4 3 2
◊ K 10
♣ 5

South
♠ A K 5
♡ K 10 8
◊ J 3
♣ A J 10 9 8

Meckstroth		Rodwell	
South	West	North	East
1 NT (a)	2 ◊	3 NT (b)	Pass
5 ♣ (c)	All Pass		

(a) 15-17

(b) Lebensohl — game-forcing with no four card major and no diamond stopper;

(c) Responder must have club support, so opener, with a near maximum, bids the "obvious" game.

The North-South pair on this deal happen to be one of the United States' finest partnerships with many championships to their credit (including the Vanderbilt in which this deal occurred.)

Five clubs was a fine contract, easily made when Meckstroth was able to get a complete count on West's hand and finesse East for the queen of hearts. In the other room West did not produce the vulnerable overcall and one notrump was raised to three notrump — two down on a diamond lead. Meckstroth and Rodwell gained 13 MPS on the deal. True, West's overcall saved the day for North-South, but, without Lebensohl, what should North bid over two diamonds? Many pairs who do not use Lebensohl might well have landed in three notrump despite the two diamond overcall.

Now let's take a look at a few more examples of Lebensohl in action:

Opener	Opponent	Responder
1 NT	2 ♠	?

♠ J 2   ♡ A J 9 7 4 2   ◇ 6 4   ♣ 6 5 3

Bid 2 Notrump. A direct three heart call would be forcing to game and you are not good enough. First you must force partner to bid three clubs by using the artificial two notrump, and then you sign off in three hearts.

Opener	Opponent	Responder
1 NT	2 ♡	?

♠ A Q J 8   ♡ A 9 8   ◇ Q 4 2   ♣ 6 4 2

Bid 2 Notrump. You want to play either in three notrump or four spades, depending upon whether or not opener has a four-card spade suit. Over opener's forced three club bid you will cue-bid three hearts (Stayman with a stopper). A direct cue-bid of three hearts over two hearts would also be game-forcing Stayman, but would deny a heart stopper. (FADS)

Opener	Opponent	Responder
1 NT	2 ♡	?

♠ K Q 7   ♡ K 8 6   ◇ A J 8 7   ♣ 10 4 3

Bid 2 Notrump. Follow with three notrump after partner's automatic three clubs. Be careful not to jump directly to three no-trump when you have a stopper in the opponents' suit, since partner will run from three notrump if he has no stopper himself. (FADS)

Opener	Opponent	Responder
1 NT	2 ♠	?

♠ 6 4 3   ♡ A Q J   ◇ A J 10 7   ♣ 10 7 6

Bid 3 Notrump. FADS. Your direct jump to three notrump lets partner know you have enough strength to be in game with no spade stopper and fewer than four hearts. If partner cannot stop the opponents' suit he will not pass three notrump.

Opener	Opponent	Responder
1 NT	2 ♠	?

♠ 9 8   ♡ A J 9 5   ◇ K Q 7 5   ♣ 10 9 8

Bid 3 Spades. You want to play in four hearts if partner has a four-card heart suit; otherwise three notrump if he can stop the spades. The direct cue-bid is Stayman without a stopper. (FADS)

Before we move on to a discussion of opener's rebids, review the basic Lebensohl response on these hands:

Partner	RHO	You
1 NT	2 ♡	?

(1) ♠ 10 9 2   ♡ 5 3   ◇ K J 10 9 7 4   ♣ 8 3

(2) ♠ 8 2   ♡ 4   ◇ A Q 10   ♣ K Q 10 9 7 4 2

(3) ♠ A Q 9 8 6   ♡ 8 6   ◇ 9 7 4   ♣ 8 7 2

(4) ♠ A Q 9 8 6   ♡ 7 5   ◇ Q 10 2   ♣ K 9 3

(5) ♠ J 10 9 8   ♡ 4 3   ◇ A Q J   ♣ Q 10 8 7

(6) ♠ Q 10 8 2   ♡ A J   ◇ 6 5 2   ♣ A 10 4 3

(7) ♠ A 9   ♡ 6 5 2   ◇ A Q 9   ♣ J 8 4 3 2

(8) ♠ A J 2   ♡ A 9   ◇ Q 9 7 6   ♣ J 10 8 3

(1) **Bid 2 Notrump.** Follow with three diamonds, signoff.

(2) **Bid 3 Clubs.** Game-force.

(3) **Bid 2 Spades.** Signoff.

(4) **Bid 3 Spades.** Game-force.

(5) **Bid 3 Hearts.** Stayman without a stopper. (FADS)

(6) **Bid 2 Notrump.** Follow with three hearts, which is Stayman with a stopper.

(7) **Bid 3 Notrump.** Game-force, no heart stopper.

(8) Bid 2 Notrump. Follow with three notrump to show a heart stopper.

OPENER'S REBIDS

Let's study the Lebensohl auction from opener's point of view. Examine the following sequences:

Opener	Opponent	Responder	Opponent
1 NT	2♡	2 NT	Pass

♠ A Q 9   ♡ K 10 5   ◇ K Q J 8 7   ♣ 3 2

Bid 3 Clubs. You have NO options! Do not be tempted to bid three diamonds because of your poor clubs. Responder may have

♠ 8 7 5   ♡ 9 8 3   ◇ —   ♣ K 10 9 8 7 6 4

Opener	Opponent	Responder	Opponent
1 NT	2 ♡	2♠	Pass

♠ J 10   ♡ K Q 9   ◇ A J 10 4   ♣ K Q J 6

Pass. Again, you have NO options. Partner wants to play in two spades. Bids at the two level are non-forcing and non-invitational. However, partner was not obliged to "improve the contract" as he would have been had your LHO passed. Therefore, he shows some moderate values; opener may raise to three spades with four-card spade support and maximum strength; e.g.

♠ A Q 10 7   ♡ 7 4   ◇ K Q 6 5   ♣ A J 10

Opener	Opponent	Responder	Opponent
1 NT	2 ♡	3♡	Pass

(1)   ♠ A 4 3 2   ♡ K 10   ◇ K J 6 5   ♣ A J 10
(2)   ♠ 8 6   ♡ K 10 7   ◇ A Q J 5   ♣ K Q J 10
(3)   ♠ A 5 3   ♡ J 6   ◇ K Q 10 8 6   ♣ A Q 2

According to Rule 5, responder's cue-bid is game-forcing Stayman promising four spades and denying a heart stopper. Therefore:

(1) Bid 3 Spades. Responder has four spades. Your first obligation is to tell him that you also have four spades. Resist the temptation to tell him about your heart stopper with three notrump. (Since your partner's bid is forcing to game, it would be incorrect for you to bid four spades, using up all the bidding room.)

(2) Bid 3 Notrump. You do not have four spades, but you do have a heart stopper.

(3) **Bid 4 Diamonds.** You do not have four spades, and you do not have a heart stopper, so you bid your long suit. Partner may pass, in which case you surely have no makeable game. Alternatively, you should consider playing the game in your 4-3 spade fit. Your hand is near-maximum and you take heart ruffs in the short trump hand.

Opener	Opponent	Responder	Opponent
1 NT	2 ♡	3 NT	Pass
?			

(1) ♠ A J 9 6   ♡ K 3   ◇ K Q 5 4   ♣ Q 10 9

(2) ♠ A J 3 2   ♡ 4 3   ◇ K Q 9 8   ♣ K Q 4

(3) ♠ A K 9 8 7   ♡ J 2   ◇ K Q 6   ♣ Q J 5

Responder's three notrump call denies four spades or a heart stopper. (FADS)

(1) **Pass.** Your heart stopper may not be very attractive, but you have little choice. Partner has denied four spades. (If he had them, he would have started with a cue-bid of three hearts — Stayman.)

(2) **Bid 4 Diamonds.** You cannot pass three notrump with a worthless doubleton heart when partner has denied a stopper. And there is little point in bidding four spades when partner also has denied four spades. Four diamonds remains as your only logical choice.

(3) **Bid 4 Spades.** Promising a five-card suit. Partner will pass if four spades looks like the best game to him.

Let's quickly review opener's options in Lebensohl sequences. Consider these hands:

You	LHO
1 NT	2 ♠

(1) **Partner bids 2 Notrump** (RHO passes)

    ♠ K Q J   ♡ A J 10 8 6   ◇ K J 10   ♣ J 2

(2) **Partner Bids 3 Notrump** (RHO passes)

    ♠ K 9 7   ♡ A Q 6 4   ◇ K Q 10   ♣ Q J 9

(3) **Partner bids 3 Spades** (RHO passes)

    ♠ K 8 6   ♡ Q 10 4 2   ◇ A Q 6   ♣ K J 4

(4) **Partner bids 3 Hearts** (RHO passes)

    ♠ A 5 4 3   ♡ A 6 2   ◇ Q J 5 3   ♣ K J

(1) **Bid 3 Clubs.** You have no choice.

(2) **Pass.** Responder has game-forcing values without four hearts. He doesn't have a spade stopper, but you do.

(3) **Bid 4 Hearts.** Responder promises four hearts and no spade stopper. Your first priority is to reveal the 4-4 fit. Ignore your spade stopper.

(4) **Bid 4 Hearts.** Partner has five or more hearts and game-forcing strength. Better to raise his suit rather than bid three notrump with only one spade stopper.

You	LHO	Partner	RHO
1 NT	2 ♡	2 NT	Pass
3 ♣	Pass		

(5) **Partner rebids 3 hearts** (RHO passes)

♠ Q 4   ♡ 8 6 5   ◇ A K Q 9   ♣ K Q 10 8

(6) **Partner rebids 3 NT** (RHO passes)

♠ K Q 10 8   ♡ 6 2   ◇ A Q 4   ♣ K Q J 10

(5) **Bid 3 Notrump.** Partner's delayed cue-bid shows four spades and promises a heart stopper.

(6) **Pass.** Responder wants to play three notrump. He has a heart stopper and he does *not* have four spades.

Not all hands will be as straightforward as the previous examples. Let's try a few tougher ones.

Opener	Opponent	Responder
1 NT	2 ♠	?

♠ K Q 10   ♡ J 5 4 3 2   ◇ Q 10 8   ♣ Q 9

Bid 2 Notrump. Plan to follow with a three spade cue-bid — theoretically showing "four" hearts and a spade stopper. This is a difficult hand. You have five hearts and game-forcing values, so, on the surface, it looks as if you should force with three hearts. But, in view of your spade holding, partner probably has no spade stopper. If he has no heart fit either, he will have to take you past your best game — three notrump. With such good spades it is best to treat your weak hearts as a four-card suit, so show your spade stoppers enroute.

Opener	Opponent	Responder	Opponent
1 NT	2 ♠	3 ♠	Pass
?			

(1)   ♠ J 3   ♡ A 10 9   ◇ A Q 6 4   ♣ K J 9 8
(2)   ♠ 5 3 2   ♡ A 6   ◇ A K J 10   ♣ K Q 10 9

Responder's cue-bid is game-forcing Stayman and denies a stopper. (FADS)

(1) **Bid 4 Clubs.** Four clubs is the least of evils in a sticky situation. Four hearts, intending to play the 4-3 fit, is a good second choice since responder is known to hold four hearts. Three notrump is out, and there's no way to give partner a choice of minors at the four level. With extra strength responder will carry on to game over four clubs.

(2) **Bid 4 Spades.** Partner should bid his better minor. You are good enough to drive to the five level and you want to reach your best trump fit.

Opener	Opponent	Responder	Opponent
1 NT	2 ♡	3 NT	Pass
?			

  (1)   ♠ K J 8 2   ♡ Q 8 6   ◇ K J 2   ♣ A Q 4

  (2)   ♠ Q 2   ♡ Q 3 2   ◇ A Q J   ♣ K Q 10 8 7

  (3)   ♠ K J 6 3   ♡ 4 3 2   ◇ K Q 8   ♣ A Q 9

  (4)   ♠ K 9 8 7 6   ♡ K 2   ◇ K J 10   ♣ A Q 10

Responder has promised sufficient values for game; he has no stopper in the heart suit, and he has denied four spades. (FADS)

(1) **Pass.** You are faced with several unpleasant choices:

    (a) play in three notrump with a tenuous heart stopper, aware that the opponents may run the suit;

    (b) bid four clubs or four diamonds with a three-card suit and hope you don't wind up in a 3-3 fit, possibly doubled;

    (c) bid four spades (promising five) in search of the 4-3 fit.

Pass seems the best of a bad lot. At worst, you'll be better placed than pairs who don't use Lebensohl. Your pass "tells" your LHO that you have a heart stopper. This may deter him from leading the suit.

(2) **Bid 4 Hearts.** Another tough problem. It could be right to pass and hope that the heart stopper will hold up. Yet three notrump may go down while six of either minor may make if partner has a singleton heart. Four clubs could even be right if partner has:

    ♠ J 2   ♡ 8   ◇ K 9 8 7 2   ♣ A 9 8 4 3

However, I believe we should make game as long as we play in the right suit. Responder may have

    ♠ A 6 4   ♡ 7 6   ◇ K 9 8 7 2   ♣ A 9 6

in which case five of either minor has reasonable play. Partner also may have

♠ A 6 4 3　♡ 7 6　◇ K 9 8 7 2　♣ A 2

and we would much rather be in five diamonds than four clubs. This deal is an excellent example of the use of the ambiguous cue-bid by opener.

(3) **Bid 4 Clubs.** Most of your notrump auctions should be a bowl of cherries, but this one has just become the pits. By bidding, you may unearth partner's five-card suit. Nothing good is likely to happen if you pass knowing that neither of you can stop the heart suit.

(4) **Pass.** Since you have only one heart stopper four spades is tempting. But partner has not promised spade length. His hand might be

♠ J 2　♡ 10 9 8　◇ A Q 8　♣ K J 9 8 7

Three notrump is excellent and four spades is virtually out of reach.

Chapter 3

GAME INVITATIONAL HANDS

So far we've looked only at hands where responder had a clear direction. He either wanted to force to game or to sign off. But what does he do when he needs an opinion from partner?

Sometimes he will have a hand where he would like to invite a game if opener has a maximum but play in a part-score if the no-trump opener is minimum.

Suppose responder picks up

♠ A 7   ♡ K J 10 9 4   ◊ 4 2   ♣ 10 9 6 3

and his RHO overcalls two diamonds after partner's one notrump opening. It would be cowardly to simply sign off in two hearts and far too ambitious to force to game. So what should responder do? In this sequence Lebensohl gives responder three ways to show his long suit:

(1) He can make a two-level bid in his suit: NON-FORCING and NON-INVITATIONAL.

(2) He can jump to the three level in his suit: FORCING TO GAME.

(3) He can relay with two notrump and then bid his suit over opener's forced three club rebid: INVITATIONAL.*

Let's try a few examples:

Opener	Opponent	Responder		
1 NT	2 ◊			
(1) ♠ 7 3	♡ A J 10 8 4	◊ 9 7 5 3	♣ 7 5	
(2) ♠ A 7	♡ K J 10 9 4	◊ 4 2	♣ 10 9 6 3	
(3) ♠ A 4	♡ A Q J 8 5	◊ 8 6 5 4	♣ 6 4	

(1) **Bid 2 Hearts.** Signoff. Opener must pass, except with a maximum opening and a fit.

---

*Note: This mechanism works only with suits higher ranking than the overcall suit. When responder's suit is lower ranking than the overcall suit he has only two ways to bid his suit. Therefore no invitational sequence is available.

(2) **Bid 2 Notrump.** Plan to bid three hearts over opener's three club rebid to invite a game if opener is maximum.

(3) **Bid 3 Hearts.** Game-forcing.

Those were quite easy. How about a tough one?

♠ 7 3   ♡ 9 8   ◊ J 10 8 2   ♣   A Q J 10 3

There is no "right" answer to this problem. You would like to invite a game after RHO's two diamond overcall, but you don't have room to do so. You will have to use your best judgment and either drive to game or stop in three clubs. I recommend starting with two notrump and then bidding three notrump over three clubs to show the diamond stopper. The club suit is good for a lot of tricks so it's probably worth a slight overbid. But if the jack of clubs were the jack of hearts, I would prefer to play in three clubs.

Try these yourself:

Partner	RHO	You
1 NT	2 ♡	?

(1) ♠ K 8 7 6 3   ♡ 4   ◊ Q J 5 2   ♣ 9 7 5

(2) ♠ K Q 10 6 3   ♡ 4   ◊ Q J 10 2   ♣ 9 7 5

(3) ♠ 8 7 2   ♡ 10 9 8   ◊ K J 10 9 4   ♣ A 10

(4) ♠ A 9 7 2   ♡ 4   ◊ J 10   ♣ K Q 10 9 8 6

(1) **Bid 2 Spades.** Signoff.

(2) **Bid 2 Notrump.** Follow with three spades, invitational.

(3) **Bid 3 Notrump.** A slight overbid but there is no invitation available (FADS).

(4) **Bid 3 Clubs.** Forcing. You can still reach four spades (if opener has four spades he will bid them). Three clubs is preferable to a cuebid sequence since five clubs or even six clubs may be your right contract. Lebensohl is meant to handle difficult hands, not straightforward hands which "bid themselves."

Chapter 4

LEBENSOHL VS. NATURAL
THREE-LEVEL OVERCALLS

Occasionally your opponents will jump to the three-level after your one notrump opening. Depending upon their agreements, this jump may show a very good hand or it may be based on a long suit with very little strength. Whatever the strength of the jump overcall, it can cause major problems since you have been denied room to exchange information.

The Lebensohl countermeasures after an enemy three-level overcall are a bit different from those employed after a two-level overcall.

**LEBENSOHL
AFTER NATURAL THREE-LEVEL OVERCALLS**

(1) A BID BELOW GAME is forcing.

(2) A DOUBLE is takeout, **not** penalty (in other words, a negative double). Opener **must** bid unless he chooses to convert the double for penalties when he has a strong trump holding.

(3) GAME BIDS are signoffs.

(4) THREE NOTRUMP shows or denies a stopper by partnership agreement. (I prefer that three notrump show a stopper and that the negative double be used on hands without a stopper, both for the sake of flexibility and ease of memory.)

(5) A CUE-BID of a minor suit is either:
    a. Stayman, or
    b. Slam interest (with or without a major).

Obviously, this structure eliminates the penalty double as a weapon in your responding arsenal. However, like negative doubles after suit openings, if responder passes, opener may elect to reopen with a double when he holds exactly two cards in the opponents' suit.

Let's study a few auctions where the opponents have over-called at the three-level. Consider responder's action in the following situations:

(Vulnerable vs. Not)

Opener	Opponent	Responder
1 NT	3 ♣	?

♠ Q 10 9 7 6　♡ A 4 3　◊ K J 8　♣ 8 5

Bid 3 Spades. Forcing. Opener will raise to four spades with support or bid three notrump with a stopper in clubs. With neither he will bid a suit of his own at the four-level.

(None Vulnerable)

Opener	Opponent	Responder
1 NT	3 ♣	?

♠ 8 5　♡ 7 4 3 2　◊ J 10 8　♣ K Q 9 8

Pass. You would like to play three clubs doubled, but a double is negative. There is no danger of missing a game if you pass, and there is a fair chance that partner will reopen with a double, as he almost certainly has two small clubs. If he does, you will happily pass for a large penalty.

(Both Vulnerable)

Opener	Opponent	Responder
1 NT	3 ♣	?

♠ A 9　♡ Q 8 3　◊ J 10 8 7　♣ K Q 9 8

Bid 3 Notrump. Double is negative, **not** penalty. If you pass, hoping for partner to reopen with a takeout double so that you can convert, you may be disappointed. Vulnerable, he may not relish the idea of putting his head on the chopping block with 15 HCP, even with two little clubs. You expect to make a game, so bid it.

(Vulnerable vs. Not)

Opener	Opponent	Responder
1 NT	3 ◇	?

♠ A 9 7 5 3   ♡ K Q 5 3   ◇ —   ♣ A J 10 7

Bid 4 Diamonds. Stayman. Plan to follow with five diamonds over any suit from opener to show your slam interest. (A negative double is not a good idea with a void in the opponent's suit, especially at this vulnerability.)

(Both Vulnerable)

Opener	Opponent	Responder
1 NT	3 ♣	?

♠ 7 6   ♡ A 4 2   ◇ 8 6 5 2   ♣ Q J 10 8

Pass. Double is negative. There is a fair chance that partner will reopen at this vulnerability. If he doesn't, there is nothing you can do about it. And you may do well enough against three clubs undoubled to get a good score.

Chapter 5

LEBENSOHL REVISITED

When playing any new convention, it's important to be thoroughly familiar with the basic principles, so let's review the critical ground we've covered in the previous chapters.

The most important concept of the Lebensohl convention is that doubles of two-level overcalls are played as penalty doubles, while doubles of three-level overcalls are "negative," showing high cards but not a trump stack.

The idea behind this is that your opponents are likely to be more careful about their three-level overcalls and you are therefore unlikely to have a trump stack. In fact, many players still treat a three-level overcall of an opponent's one notrump as a very powerful playing hand. This makes it even less likely that you will want to make a penalty double. More importantly, if you have a balanced hand, it is much harder to bid at the three-level without using the negative double because there is so little bidding space left.

(None Vulnerable)

Opener	Opponent	Responder
1 NT	2 ♡	?

(1) ♠ A 9   ♡ Q J 8 6   ◇ J 10 9 5   ♣ 10 9 2

(2) ♠ A Q 10 9   ♡ 4 3 2   ◇ Q 10 9 5   ♣ 9 8

(1) **Double.** An easy bid. This could be a serious beating while your side may not even have a game.

(2) **Bid 2 Spades (?).** Not so easy. Double is penalty so that's out. Pass is not an option when you know that your side has at least 23 HCP. Two spades shows five spades and does not invite game. Two notrump is Lebensohl and you have no follow-up. Three hearts (Stayman) is a possibility but will get you to a very light game unless you violate your agreements and pass partner's possible three spade call. I would choose two spades only because I'm caught "between a rock and a hard place." Nothing has much to recommend it, and whatever action you take may not meet with great success.

(Both Vulnerable)

Opener	Opponent	Responder
1 NT	3 ♣	?

♠ A J 9 8   ♡ K 10 8 7   ◊ K 9 8 6   ♣ J

Double. A perfect "negative" double. You are ready for any suit opener bids; if he converts the double for penalties, you will be happy to defend.

(Non-Vulnerable vs. Vulnerable)

Opener	Opponent	Responder
1 NT	3 ♣	?

♠ A J 9 8   ♡ K 4 2   ◊ K 9 7 4   ♣ J 8

Double. No longer perfect, but still quite acceptable. If you're lucky, opener will rebid three spades or three notrump. (If you're very lucky he'll pass!) If he bids three diamonds or three hearts you'll have to scramble with three spades (forcing). But you won't land in three notrump with no stopper, and you may be able to reach a good 4-3 major fit.

(Vulnerable vs. Not)

Opener	Opponent	Responder
1 NT	3 ◊	?

♠ K Q 6 4   ♡ A J 5 2   ◊ —   ♣ 10 9 6 5 3

Bid 4 Diamonds. Stayman. This is similar to the previous examples. With no diamonds, it's not a good idea to risk a negative double, especially at this vulnerability — if partner passes you can be fairly sure that he's wrong. You will have a hard time collecting enough to compensate for the likely game you've missed.

What do you do in each of the following situations?

Partner	RHO	You
1 NT	2 ♡	?

(1) ♠ Q 10 9   ♡ K 10 8 7   ◇ Q J 8   ♣ 10 9 7

(2) ♠ Q 10 9 8   ♡ K 10   ◇ Q J 8 3   ♣ J 10 9

(3) ♠ 7 5   ♡ J 7 4 3   ◇ K Q J 9 7   ♣ 4 2

(4) ♠ A 7 6   ♡ K 9   ◇ Q 10 5 4   ♣ Q 5 3 2

(1) **Double.** Penalty. The opponents are in trouble. Make them pay for the foolish overcall.

(2) **Bid 2 Notrump.** Follow with three hearts. Stayman with a stopper. Double is a penalty at the two-level, **not** negative.

(3) **Bid 2 Notrump.** Follow with three diamonds, signoff. Don't make a penalty double with bad trumps and all of your high cards in your long suit. If partner has a diamond fit your opponents will make overtricks.

(4) **Bid 2 Notrump.** Follow with three notrump. It's a losing business to double without good trumps — even with a lot of high cards.

Partner	RHO	You
1 NT	3 ◇	?

(5) ♠ A 10   ♡ 7 3 2   ◇ Q 10 9 4   ♣ 9 8 7 4

(6) ♠ A 7 6 2   ♡ 7 3   ◇ Q 10 9 4   ♣ A 8 3

(7) ♠ K J 9 8 6   ♡ 8   ◇ A 10 3   ♣ Q J 9 3

(5) **Pass.** Double is negative at the three-level. Of course you hope partner reopens. If he doesn't, you haven't missed a game, and you will certainly go plus against three diamonds.

(6) **Double.** Negative. Too good to pass and hope partner will reopen. Best to search for a spade or notrump game (if partner rebids three hearts over your double).

(7) **Bid 3 Spades.** Forcing. Don't make a negative double with a five-card major. Partner will not bid a three-card suit and the fit will be lost.

Now let's look at things from opener's point of view after responder has doubled.

(None Vulnerable)

(a)

Opener	Opponent	Responder	Opponent
1 NT	3 ♡	Double	Pass
?			

♠ Q 10 8 7   ♡ A 4 3   ◇ A Q 6   ♣ K J 10

Bid 3 Spades. Your partner is most likely to have four spades for his negative double. Do not be tempted to bid three notrump with only one heart stopper when you have four spades. Without a source of tricks, three notrump probably won't be a good contract anyway.

(None Vulnerable)

(b)

Opener	Opponent	Responder	Opponent
1 NT	3 ◇	Pass	Pass
?			

(1)   ♠ K Q J 8   ♡ K Q 10 9   ◇ 10 8   ♣ A J 10

(2)   ♠ K J 9 4   ♡ K Q 4 2   ◇ J 3   ♣ A J 9

(1) **Double.** Protect partner in case he has a penalty double of three diamonds. If not, you have a **very** good hand and can probably manage a three-level contract even when responder doesn't have much.

(2) **Pass.** Double is too risky with such a skimpy minimum. True, partner may have a penalty double of three diamonds, but you can't afford to take the risk. If you catch him with a bad hand, you'll need an ambulance!

The following deal is a nice illustration of the importance of the three-level negative double by responder.

West Dealer
North-South Vulnerable

North
♠ K 6 5
♡ A 10 8
♢ 6 3
♣ A K Q 6 2

West
♠ 9 4 3 2
♡ 7 5 4 3
♢ 4
♣ 9 8 5 4

East
♠ Q J 10 8
♡ 6 2
♢ A K Q J 8 5
♣ 10

South
♠ A 7
♡ K Q J 9
♢ 10 9 7 2
♣ J 7 3

	Andersen		Benaroya
West	North	East	South
Pass	1 NT	3 ♢	Double*
Pass	4 ♣	Pass	4 ♡
All Pass			

* Negative

When this deal occurred, Alan Benaroya and I were on our way to winning the event. Most North-South pairs were defeated in three notrump when East passed, hoping to defend a notrump contract. Many pairs reached five clubs after the overcall and made it easily. However, + 650 in four hearts was worth 23 out of 25 matchpoints. Without the negative double our fate would probably have been the same as those who went down in three notrump, even with the overcall! With ♢ 10 9 7 2, Allan would have tried three notrump in hopes of finding me with at least doubleton jack, and we would have been − 200 along with most of the field. Note that a penalty double scores 500 points at most, a little over average on the board. Clearly, the negative double was indispensable on this deal.

QUIZ ON PART I

This quiz is designed to challenge your new skills with Lebensohl. Many of the problems are tough and some of the suggested solutions may not be clearcut.

Partner	RHO	You
1 NT	2 ♡	?

What action do you take with each of these hands?

(1) None Vulnerable
♠ J 10 8 5 3   ♡ 8 5   ◊ K J 3   ♣ 9 5 2

(2) None Vulnerable
♠ J 10 9 4 3   ♡ 8 4   ◊ K J 2   ♣ K 7 5

(3) None Vulnerable
♠ J 10 9 6 5 4   ♡ K 3   ◊ A Q J   ♣ K 8

(4) None Vulnerable
♠ K J 10 8 6   ♡ 6 4   ◊ A Q J 4   ♣ K 2

(5) Both Vulnerable
♠ 6 3   ♡ 9 8   ◊ K 7 6   ♣ Q 10 9 5 4 3

(6) Both Vulnerable
♠ A 3   ♡ 8 5   ◊ K 3 2   ♣ K Q 10 9 6 5

(7) Both Vulnerable
♠ 4 2   ♡ 9 6   ◊ K 8 4   ♣ K Q 10 9 7 5

(8) Vulnerable vs. Not
♠ Q 6 4   ♡ 9 7 6   ◊ A Q 2   ♣ K 8 6 5

(9) Vulnerable vs. Not
♠ 6 5 4   ♡ K 7 6   ◊ A Q 3   ♣ K 9 4 3

(10) Vulnerable vs. Not
♠ Q 8 4 2   ♡ 5 3   ◊ A Q 3   ♣ K 8 6 3

(11) Vulnerable vs. Not
♠ Q 9 6 4   ♡ Q 4 2   ◊ A Q 2   ♣ K 8 7

(12) Both Vulnerable
♠ A 9 8 6   ♡ Q 6 5 4   ◊ J 4 3   ♣ 3 2

ANSWERS

(1) **Bid 2 Spades.** Non-forcing and non-invitational.

(2) **Bid 2 Notrump.** Plan to follow with three spades, invitational.

(3) **Bid 3 Spades.** Forcing.

(4) **Bid 3 Spades.** A six-card suit is not necessary for a jump.

(5) **Bid 2 Notrump.** Pass opener's three club rebid.

(6) **Bid 3 Clubs.** Forcing.

(7) **Bid 3 Clubs.** There is no invitational sequence available, thus the game-forcing overbid. Three notrump, denying a stopper, is also acceptable; but if opener has to pull three notrump, he will almost certainly bid past four clubs. Therefore, three clubs is preferable.

(8) **Bid 3 Notrump.** FADS.

(9) **Bid 2 Notrump.** And then three notrump to show a stopper.

(10) **Bid 3 Hearts.** Stayman without a stopper. FADS.

(11) **Bid 2 Notrump.** Follow with three hearts. Stayman with a stopper.

(12) **Double.** Penalty. Not enough strength to look for a four-four spade fit.

Partner	RHO	You
1 NT	3 ◇	?

What do you do with

(13) Both Vulnerable
♠ A J 10 4   ♡ K 3   ◇ 7 5 4   ♣ Q 7 6 2

(14) Both Vulnerable
♠ K 6   ♡ A J 10 7   ◇ 9 8 5   ♣ Q 9 8 5

(15) Both Vulnerable
♠ A 9 6 2   ♡ K 9 8 5   ◇ —   ♣ J 9 6 5 3

(16) Both Vulnerable
♠ A 6 4 2   ♡ K Q 6 3   ◇ —   ♣ A J 8 5 4

(17) Both Vulnerable
♠ J 8 7   ♡ 9 6 5 3   ◇ K 10 7 6   ♣ Q 4

(18) Both Vulnerable
♠ A J 2   ♡ 7 6 5 4   ◇ K 10 4 3   ♣ Q 3

ANSWERS

(13) **Double.** Negative. Bid three spades over opener's possible three heart rebid.

(14) **Double.** Bid three notrump if opener rebids three spades. Does **not** promise a stopper.

(15) **Double.** Risky with a diamond void, but you do not have enough to gamble a game. If partner passes, you should usually expect to beat three diamonds.

(16) **Bid 4 Diamonds.** Too good to risk a pass of three diamonds doubled.

(17) **Pass.** Must hope partner will reopen with a double.

(18) **Bid 3 Notrump.** Don't risk a pass-out by partner with game-forcing values.

How does Lebensohl work when you play a weak notrump? Here are a few examples:

Partner	RHO	You
1 NT*	2 ♠	?

*12-14 HCP

What do you bid with

(19) None Vulnerable

♠ 7 5 ♡ A 9 2 ◊ Q J 6 5 4 3 ♣ Q 4

(20) None Vulnerable

♠ Q 4 ♡ A J 9 8 3 ◊ Q J 9 3 ♣ 4 2

(21) None Vulnerable

♠ 4 3 ♡ A J 9 8 5 ◊ Q J 5 4 ♣ K 8

(22) None Vulnerable

♠ K 10 7 ♡ A Q 9 6 ◊ K 10 5 2 ♣ 7 3

(23) None Vulnerable

♠ K 10 6 ♡ A 9 5 2 ◊ K 10 8 7 ♣ 9 5

(24) Both Vulnerable

♠ K J 10 2 ♡ 9 4 3 ◊ 6 5 4 2 ♣ 8 6

ANSWERS

(19) **Bid 2 Notrump.** Sign off in three diamonds over opener's three club rebid.

(20) **Bid 2 Notrump.** Sign off in three hearts. No invitational bid available and not enough to force to game. The queen of spades is probably not a working card anyway.

(21) **Bid 3 Hearts.** Game-forcing. An overbid, but preferable to signing off with all working values.

(22) **Bid 2 Notrump.** Follow with three spades. Stayman with a stopper.

(23) **Double.** Penalty. Not enough strength to force to game and no invitational bid is available.

(24) **Pass.** Double is tempting, but the opponents have 22-24 HCP and can very likely take nine tricks in another suit. Pass and hope they play in two spades which is their worst spot.

Chapter 6

LEBENSOHL AFTER ARTIFICIAL OVERCALLS

If you are a duplicate player, you've undoubtedly encountered many pairs using exotic gadgets over your notrump openings. Armed with everything from Landy to Crash, they jump into the auction to describe one-suited, two-suited and three-suited hands. The general idea behind this barrage of gadgets is to get in your way. Clearly, you need some ammunition of your own to cope with them.

In most cases you can use a basic Lebensohl, just as you would if the overcall were natural. Usually you will find yourself in reasonably good position to handle whatever happens.

However, the nuisance bid will sometimes give you a headache. For example, if you don't know what suit(s) the opponents have, how do you know what suit to cue-bid? And how do you make a penalty double if they haven't yet bid the suit they have? What about those artificial doubles showing a one-suiter? How do you tell partner you want to double? And how do you use Stayman and Jacoby?

Before we answer some of those questions, glance at the list below. It should help you to recognize most of the conventions you are likely to come up against:

Astro	Hamilton
Becker	Landy
Brozel	Pinpoint Astro
Cappelletti	Ripstra
Crash	

A few general rules about Lebensohl versus artificial bids first and then we'll take a look at the conventions you'll face most often.

LEBENSOHL VS. ARTIFICIAL OVERCALLS AND DOUBLES

(1) Vs. TWO-SUITERS WHERE BOTH SUITS ARE KNOWN (e.g. Landy, Ripstra, Brozel): The cheaper cue-bid is

game invitational; the higher cue-bid forces to game. **All Lebensohl rules are on:** Two-level bids are to play, three-level bids are forcing, two notrump transfers to three clubs, etc. A sequence of one notrump — two hearts (for majors) — two notrump by you — three clubs by partner — three diamonds by you shows a weak hand with long diamonds, while an immediate bid of three diamonds after the two heart overcall is strong and forcing.

(2) Vs. TWO-SUITERS WHERE ONE OR BOTH SUITS ARE UNKNOWN (e.g. Astro, Crash): The known suit is the cue-bid and **all basic Lebensohl principles apply.** (If you don't know either of their suits, you have no cue-bid available.)

(3) CUE-BIDS are Stayman-like in nature (unless the overcall showed both majors), and generally game-forcing. (See Rule 1 for exception.)

(4) DELAYED CUE-BIDS (after two notrump relay) show or deny stoppers by partnership agreement.

(5) FOUR-LEVEL JUMPS retain their normal meaning (as if there had been no overcall). FOUR-LEVEL NON-JUMPS are natural game-forces (or cue-bids).

(6) DOUBLES and REDOUBLES are natural. Double promises defensive values in one or both of the opponents' suits. Opener is invited to double anything he can. Redouble shows a good hand.

(7) DELAYED DOUBLES (after an initial pass) are penalty. DELAYED SUIT BIDS are simply competitive.

(8) Vs. ARTIFICIAL DOUBLES: Ignore them! Two clubs is Stayman and all other bids are as if RHO had passed. (**No Lebensohl needed.***)

(9) Vs. ARTIFICIAL TWO CLUBS SHOWING AN UN-SPECIFIED ONE-SUITER: Double is Stayman, otherwise ignore the overcall. (**No Lebensohl needed.***)

---

*Several modern defenses vs. one notrump utilize conventional doubles or two club overcalls to describe one-suited hands. The countermeasure used successfully by most experts to combat these artificial competitive tools is to simple IGNORE THEM! If a two club overcall shows some one-suiter, double now becomes Stayman.

(10) PASS is forcing. If partner of the overcaller passes the conventional takeout (other than an artificial double), the notrump opener must reopen the auction (with either a cooperative double or redouble or a bid of a five-card or longer suit).

Let's take a look at Lebensohl in action against some of the more common conventions:

Lebensohl Vs. Landy

A two club overcall by an opponent is takeout for the majors. Following the basic rules for auctions where we know both of the opponents' suits:

- Two hearts is a game-invitational cue-bid and two spades is a game-forcing cue-bid.

- If your hand is defensively oriented, you can double for penalties (showing at least one major, **not** clubs).

- Two diamonds is to play.

- Three clubs and three diamonds are forcing.

- Two notrump is Lebensohl and starts an invitational sequence in diamonds or a signoff in clubs (as well as delayed cue-bids).

- Jumps to three hearts and three spades are undefined. (You can assign your own meanings or simply agree that these bids don't exist!)

What action should you take after a Landy two club overcall of partner's opening one notrump with each of the following hands?

(Both Vulnerable)

♠ 5 3　♡ 5 4 2　♦ 9 7　♣ K Q 9 7 5 4

Bid 2 Notrump. Lebensohl, planning to pass opener's forced three club rebid.

(None Vulncrable)

♠ 9 6　♡ 7 5 4　◊ K Q 4 2　♣ A 6 3 2

Bid 2 Hearts. Invitational cue-bid, planning to pass opener's two notrump, three club or three diamond rebid. (With a maximum opener and major-suit stoppers, partner should bid game.)

(Vulnerable vs. Not)

♠ 9 7　♡ K 5 3　◊ K Q 9 8　♣ A 6 5 3

Bid 2 Notrump. Follow with three hearts (or three spades) to show (or deny) a stopper (by partnership agreement).

(None Vulnerable)

♠ A 10 7 2　♡ Q 9 5 4　◊ J 8 5　♣ 9 8

Double. Penalty. You will be happy to double either major. (You are not promising defense against clubs.)

(Vulnerable vs. Not)

♠ 5 3　♡ 8 7 5　◊ A Q 10 3　♣ K Q J 7

Bid 2 Spades. Game-forcing cue-bid. (Two-level cue-bids say nothing about stoppers.)

(None Vulnerable)

♠ Q 5　♡ 5 4 3　◊ A Q 7 6 4 3　♣ 8 2

Bid 2 Notrump. Follow with three diamonds, invitational.

(Both Vulnerable)

♠ A Q 10 4　♡ 9 3　◊ K 6 4 3　♣ J 7 5

Double. You are happy to double two spades. Invite partner to double two hearts.

(None Vulnerable)

♠ 9 8　♡ 3　◊ K 7 6　♣ A Q 10 7 5 3 2

Bid 3 Clubs. Natural and forcing. Don't muddy the waters with a double of two clubs. Double is a penalty double of one or both majors, **not** clubs.

Lebensohl Vs. Becker, Ripstra et al

Many of your opponents will be using their conventional take-out showing the majors. Becker utilizes two diamonds rather than two clubs; Ripstra employs better minor, two clubs or two diamonds. Crash often appropriates the two diamond bid as well to show both majors. Whatever the name of the treatment, your approach should be the same as that which you use against Landy.

Lebensohl Vs. Astro

A two club overcall by the opponents shows hearts and an unspecified minor. Similarly, a two diamond overcall shows spades and an unknown second suit.

After a two club Astro overcall:

- Two hearts is game-forcing Stayman.

- Two diamonds and two spades are to play.

- Three clubs, three diamonds and three spades are natural and forcing.

- Two notrump is Lebensohl.

- Three hearts is undefined. (I like to use it as a splinter.)

- Double is penalty of hearts.

Can you figure out what action to take after a two diamond overcall (Astro) with each of these hands?

(Both Vulnerable)

♠ A 6　♡ Q J 10 3　◇ Q 9 7　♣ K 7 4 3

Bid 2 Spades. Cue-bid, Stayman. (Or two notrump followed by three spades if that's the way you and your partner have agreed to show a spade stopper with four hearts.)

(Both Vulnerable)

♠ K 3 2　♡ 7 5 4　◇ Q 10 9 4 3 2　♣ 5

Bid 2 Notrump. Follow with three diamonds, signoff, after partner bids three clubs. You cannot double two diamonds; that promises a good hand with defensive values against spades — the suit your RHO showed. Three diamonds directly over two diamonds is natural and game-forcing, so you must start with two notrump, Lebensohl.

Lebensohl vs. Brozel

The Brozel convention uses a double of one notrump to show a one-suited hand. The partner of the doubler is expected to remove the double to two clubs to enable the doubler to show his suit.

The Brozel double need not cause you any problem whatsoever. Follow the basic approach over artificial doubles — simply IGNORE it. Whatever methods your partnership normally employs are still in effect (Stayman, Jacoby, etc.). The double has also given you a redouble which you would not normally have available. I suggest that you use it to penalize the opponents. For example:

Partner	RHO	You
1 NT	Double*	?

*Brozel (one-suiter)

(a) ♠ 7 5 2   ♡ Q 10 8 6   ◇ K J 6 2   ♣ A 9

(b) ♠ Q 10 9 8 7   ♡ A 4 3   ◇ 4   ♣ 10 8 7 4

(c) ♠ A 4   ♡ 10 8   ◇ A Q 10 8 7 6   ♣ 9 8 4

(a) **Redouble.** If RHO has one of the red suits you want to make a penalty double.

(b) **Bid 2 Spades.** (Or two hearts if you play Jacoby transfers.) Just bid what you would have if RHO had passed.

(c) **Bid 3 Notrump.** Make the same bid you would have made had RHO passed.

If you encounter any other kind of artificial double of one notrump, treat it the same way, i.e., ignore it unless you wish to redouble for penalties. For example, many players use some variation of Crash vs. one notrump, where double shows two unknown suits. Unless you wish to double the opponents when they reach a contract in one of their suits, you simply bid as if the double had not occurred.

Lebensohl Vs. Two Clubs Showing an Unspecified One-Suiter

This treatment has many names depending upon the part of the country in which you play, for instance Hamilton or Cappalletti. Whatever the name, a two club overcall shows a long suit, not necessarily clubs; two diamonds, two hearts and two spades are used to show various two-suiters. You can easily deal with these following the basic rules for Lebensohl after artificial bids.

After the two club overcall, the partner of the overcaller is expected to bid two diamonds so that the two club bidder can pass or name his suit.

Following the basic principles prescribed for this type of interference, your general approach should be to IGNORE the two club call. A double of two clubs is Stayman, but everything else carries the same meaning that it would have if RHO had not bid. Your only problem occurs when you want to make a penalty double. For example:

Partner	RHO	You
1 NT	2♣*	?

*Artificial, one-suited

(None Vulnerable)

♠ K J 3   ♡ A 10 4 3   ◇ K 9   ♣ Q 10 8 6

Your side can certainly take at least eight tricks against anything except two diamonds for an excellent score. But you can't double because double is Stayman, and partner will bid. The solution is to pass now and double on the next round. If you recall two of the fundamental rules, you shouldn't have any problem with this interference:

(1) The delayed double is 100 % penalty.

(2) Responder's pass is forcing on opener if the partner of the two club bidder should happen to pass, as he occasionally does when he has a bad hand with long clubs.

With this hand, the worst that can happen to you if you pass is that your LHO will bid two diamonds which gets passed around to you. In that case you can't double since double is for penalties. But you can reopen with a three diamond cue-bid (forcing to game), telling partner that you have a good hand. He should be able to figure out what you hold, since you didn't bid the first time.

(Both Vulnerable)

♠ 5 4   ♡ 8 7   ◇ A J 9 4   ♣ A 10 8 6 5

You think your RHO's long suit is one of the majors — but you could be wrong. It doesn't hurt to wait one round before signing off in clubs. Pass and await developments. If, as you expect, they escape to two hearts or two spades, you can compete with three clubs. If they should happen to land in a minor suit, you can double on the second round. (Remember that pass followed by a double is 100% penalty.)

♠ K Q J 6 5   ♡ Q 9 8   ◇ J 3 2   ♣ 9 2

If you play Jacoby transfers after your one notrump openings, you would bid two hearts with this hand, planning to follow with two notrump invitational. After the artificial two club overcall you can take the same action. Ignore the overcall and bid two hearts to transfer to two spades.

♠ Q 5 4   ♡ K 8   ◇ Q J 10 8 7   ♣ 4 3 2

You would have bid two notrump over partner's one notrump opening, so go ahead and bid it. Don't worry about your three small clubs — your RHO may not have that suit. Remember that two clubs was artificial.

(Vulnerable vs. Not)

♠ K 9 6 4   ♡ Q 8 7 5   ◇ 2   ♣ A 5 3 2

You can be reasonably sure that RHO's suit is diamonds, and you are not interested in defending two diamonds doubled at this vulnerability. You would like to bid Stayman. Remember how? A double of the two club overcall is Stayman.

Lebensohl Vs. Two Clubs and Two Diamonds Showing Unspecified Two-Suiters

Again, following the basic rules, two clubs doesn't give you any problem. Double is Stayman, everything else is normal, and pass followed by double is penalty.

However, two diamonds does present you with a problem because you've lost a little bidding room. We suggest using double as Stayman, just as you would over two clubs. Again, it follows that pass followed by a later double is for penalties (with the pass forcing, of course). In addition, we advise that basic Lebensohl principles function (two-level to play, three-level forcing, etc.). However, you have no cue-bid since you don't know which suits the opponents are bidding. Fortunately, the cue-bid is not really necessary when you use double as Stayman. And you will frequently find that double works out better on hands where you would like to cue-bid because it can be converted for penalties.

* * * * * * * *

Before we leave this topic, a word to the wise is in order. We have seen that responder's double indicates a desire to defend against the suit(s) **shown**, not the suit **bid**. Therefore, common sense dictates that you apply two fundamental strategies in doubling the opponents when they make a conventional overcall in a suit they may not have:

> (1) Responder should avoid doubling with a singleton or void in the suit bid. LHO may have the suit or it may be RHO's unknown suit. Even if partner has four trumps, it is not at all clear that you want to defend at the two-level when the opponents have a eight-card fit.

> (2) Opener should not pass out responder's double of the artificial bid (after his RHO has passed) without a fairly good holding in the suit doubled — generally four trumps or three very good ones; Qxx **may** be sufficient if his hand is very strong defensively; a doubleton is **never** enough to pass!

Chapter 7

LEBENSOHL INNOVATIONS

The standard Lebensohl methods we've been discussing will greatly improve the bidding accuracy of most partnerships. These tools have the added advantages of

(1) Being relatively simple to remember;

(2) Clarifying which responses are signoff, invitational or game forcing;

(3) Clarifying when responder has a stopper in the enemy suit and when he does not.

For most of you, Lebensohl as it has been presented up to this point will be more than adequate and will bring you many more good results than you are currently obtaining. However, for those partnerships with a more scientific bent, once you have had some practice with the basic principles involved, you may want to consider some of the recent modifications to the basic structure. These treatments are used to good advantage by many experts in the handling of the more difficult hands.

FASS

You may recall that the procedure set forth in an earlier chapter for showing or denying a stopper in the enemy suit is commonly known by its acronym "FADS" — Fast Auction Denies Stopper. This alludes to its fundamental structure: the direct (or "fast") cue-bid and the direct jump to three notrump deny a stopper, while the slower auction incorporating the two notrump relay shows a stopper.

This entire mechanism can easily be reversed so that the faster auction shows the stopper (FASS), and the slower auction denies the stopper.

There are a couple of advantages to FASS which you might want to consider:

(1) FASS is probably easier to remember in some auctions. After one notrump - two spades (overcall), responder's jump to three notrump has a very natural ring to it. Using FADS, it is not at all difficult to imagine that either opener or responder might forget that the jump to three notrump denies a stopper. On the other hand, if you use FASS principles, the jump to three notrump promises a stopper in the enemy suit — just the way it sounds!

(2) When you don't have a stopper, it is very possible that you can't make a game even with sufficient high cards. If your conventional agreements with such hands allow you to go slowly — i.e., to start with two notrump — it is possible that your opponents will foolishly bid again, allowing you to make a penalty double — for your only available plus score. If you use FADS you will have to cue-bid or jump to three notrump immediately, thereby depriving the enemy of the opportunity to fall into a trap.

There is one serious flaw with FASS: when you have a scanty holding in overcaller's suit, it's likely that his partner will be able to compete to the three-level. Now you lose your Stayman sequences and other auctions will become much more complex.

Negative Doubles

What is the correct bid after one notrump — two spades when your hand is:

♠ A 8   ♡ Q 10 8 6   ◇ J 10 7 6   ♣ 9 8 5   ?

You certainly don't like to pass when your side has between 22 and 24 HCP, but you can't force to game with only 7 HCP and no five-card suit. You do not have a long suit where you can sign off or invite. And you surely can't make a penalty double with only two spades.

In fact, using standard Lebensohl you cannot handle this hand at all. If you remember, the bid we gave up in order to play Lebensohl was the natural two notrump — the bid you would have made with this sort of hand in the old days.

The solution found by tournament players is to employ negative doubles after a one notrump opener, just as you do when you open one of a suit. With the hand above you would double, showing competitive values and support for the other three suits.

You should take a few precautions if you decide to try negative doubles after partner opens one notrump. I suggest:

(1) Play negative doubles through three spades.

(2) Never make a negative double with game-forcing values unless you don't mind hearing partner pass.

(3) Don't use negative doubles over artificial or conventional bids.

(4) Don't make a negative double without at least close to game-invitational values.

(5) If partner does not double or bid, opener **must** reopen at the two-level if he has only two small cards in the opponents' suit, to protect against the possibility responder wanted to make a penalty double. He should consider reopening with any doubleton. And he should also consider reopening at the three-level with two small cards in the opponents' suit.

What would you bid after one notrump—two spades?

(Vulnerable vs. Not)

♠ 4   ♡ Q 10 9 6   ◇ A Q 6 4   ♣ K 7 3 2

Bid 3 Spades. At this vulnerability you cannot afford to risk a negative double, especially when you have a singleton spade. If you make a negative double and partner passes, chances are you won't collect a large enough penalty to compensate for the game you've missed.

(Vulnerable vs. Not)

♠ 6 5   ♡ Q 10 8 7   ◇ A Q 4 3   ♣ 7 5 2

Double. Whether partner bids or passes, you will be happy with his decision. (After all, you weren't planning to bid game.) Remember that he will pass only if he holds good spades, especially at this vulnerability.

(Both Vulnerable)

♠ 4 2   ♡ A J 3   ◇ 8 7 5 3 2   ♣ Q J 9

Double. You are not required to have four hearts for a negative double. Even though you have a five-card suit, I like the negative double because it is a more flexible approach. This is especially true when your suit is so bad.

Lebensohl vs. Landy

Unfortunately, many players "accidentally" bid two clubs with clubs when they are playing Landy. This can cause you some difficulty if you don't wish to double and risk defending two clubs. More important, it is not surprising to find that an opponent has made a Landy call with something like 9 6 5 3 in one of the majors — often the one you want to play!

For these reasons you may wish to forget cue-bids altogether. Many of today's expert players who play Lebensohl treat all major suit bids, after an opponent's Landy call, as **natural.** Two hearts and two spades are to play. Three hearts and three spades are natural and forcing, and two notrump followed by three hearts and three spades are natural and invitational. If you adopt this treatment, you can still use a double of two clubs for penalties of one or both majors. The advantage of this approach is that when you hold an offensive hand with a major suit, either weak or strong, you have a straightforward way to bid it.

Opener	RHO	You
1 NT	2 ♣*	?

*Landy

(None Vulnerable)

(a)   ♠ Q 9 7 4   ♡ A 8   ◇ K 6 4 3   ♣ 8 7 2

(Both Vulnerable)

(b)   ♠ Q J 9 8 6 5   ♡ A 4   ◇ 9 8 6   ♣ 4 2

(None Vulnerable)

(c)   ♠ Q J 9 8 5 2   ♡ 5 3   ◇ 8 7 3   ♣ 8 7

(Vulnerable vs Not)

(d)   ♠ K Q 10 8 5 4   ♡ —   ◇ A 9 3 2   ♣ Q 9 8

(a) **Double.** Penalty, major suit oriented. You would be happy to double two spades, and you'd like to hear partner double two hearts if he can.

(b) **Bid 2 Notrump.** Lebensohl. Follow with three spades, invitational. Don't waste time and cloud the issue with a double. You have no intention of defending anything but spades and there is little chance of that turn of events when they have at most five spades between them.

(c) **Bid 2 Spades.** To play. Again, there is no point in a double. You don't plan to defend anything doubled, so don't invite partner to double.

(d) **Bid 3 Spades.** Forcing. You may even have a spade slam. You must show your suit before they bid a lot of hearts if you are to have any hope of an intelligent auction.

Should you decide to try this approach against your opponents' Landy calls, you will find it an equally effective treatment after other artificial two club and two diamond takeout bids by the opponents (showing the majors).

Lebensohl With Jacoby

Another Lebensohl refinement often attractive to tournament players is the incorporation of Jacoby transfers.

This may take any form you and your partner prefer. One suggested approach is:

After an overcall of partner's notrump opener:

(1) Bids at the two-level are natural and non-forcing. (No change from standard Lebensohl.)

(2) Two notrump transfers to three clubs.
Three clubs transfers to three diamonds.
Three diamonds transfers to three hearts.
Three hearts transfers to three spades.

(3) A transfer to the opponents' suit is Stayman, with exactly the same meaning as one notrump — two hearts — three hearts in basic Lebensohl. For instance, the sequence one notrump — two hearts — three diamonds would show a four-card spade suit and deny a stopper, since you didn't use the two notrump relay before you cue-bid.

(4) If there is room, you can transfer and then show a stopper by cue-bidding: one notrump — two spades (overcall) — three clubs (transfer to

diamonds) — three diamonds — three spades (cue-bid) shows a long diamond suit with a spade stopper.

There are two, perhaps insignificant, advantages in combining transfers with Lebensohl:

> (1) The notrump opener declares, preventing a lead through a holding such as K x in the opponent's suit.

> (2) Some constructive auctions will be easier; e.g., after one notrump - two spades:

> If responder has six diamonds and four hearts he can transfer to three diamonds (with a three club bid), then bid three hearts, forcing — clarifying his hand at the lowest possible level.

The same principles apply as when using basic Lebensohl — if you make a negative double and then rebid three notrump, you have a stopper in the opponent's suit; if you bid three notrump immediately, you do not have a stopper. Naturally, you have to be prepared for any bid that partner can make.

Whatever their merit, many experts do merge Jacoby transfers with Lebensohl in competition. You may wish to give them a try.

Two Notrump for Better Minor

Quite a useful improvement on the fundamental Lebensohl framework is the use of two notrump as an inquiry, asking opener to bid his better minor.

This allows responder to compete effectively after a two heart or two spade overcall with hands like

♠ 6 3   ♡ 4 3   ◇ A Q 10 4   ♣ J 7 5 4 2, or

♠ 7   ♡ 7 6   ◇ J 9 8 6 5   ♣ A 10 9 5 2,

where negative doubles won't help. Using the standard Lebensohl approach, his only choice with such a hand is to pick a suit to play at the three-level and hope he is guessing well that day. Obviously, this hit-or-miss approach can easily strand the partnership in a poor seven-card fit when there is an eight or nine-card fit available elsewhere. However, if responder has "two notrump for better minor" at his disposal, he is able to ask opener which minor he prefers.

If you and your partner elect to try this, you will need to clarify a few points about responder's bids:

(1) Three clubs is to play — non-forcing and non-invitational.

(2) Three diamonds, three hearts and three spades are natural and forcing.

(3) To sign off in three diamonds, start with two notrump, asking for better minor. If opener chooses three clubs, correct to three diamonds — non-forcing and non-invitational.

(4) After a two diamond overcall, two notrump remains a transfer to three clubs. (Better minor applies only after a two-of-a-major overcall.)

(5) Two notrump followed by a three-level cue-bid in the opponents' suit is Stayman with a stopper (or Stayman without a stopper if you use FASS).

(6) To force in clubs you must start with either two notrump or a cue-bid; or you can jump to four clubs if that is natural in your style.

If you've chosen to adopt the "two notrump for better minor" mechanism, you may wish to go one step further and add Jacoby transfers at the three-level. The two combine quite well. You need make only one or two minor changes in the structure outlined above:

(1) Three clubs is to play.
Three diamonds transfers to three hearts.
Three hearts transfers to three spades.
Three spades transfers to four clubs.
Four clubs transfers to four diamonds.

(2) Transfer to opponents' suit = "fast" cue-bid.

All other bids retain the same meaning as in the basic "two notrump for better minor" structure.

The deal below, played in an ACBL Regional, is a good example of the usefulness of "two notrump for better minor."

North-South Vulnerable
East Dealer

                            North
                            ♠ 9 2
                            ♡ —
                            ◇ 9 7 5 4 3
                            ♣ Q 10 9 7 5 4

        West   East
        ♠ Q 10 6 3   ♠ J 8 7 5
        ♡ K Q J 9 7 6   ♡ A 4 3 2
        ◇ 2   ◇ Q J
        ♣ A J   ♣ 8 6 3

                            South
                            ♠ A K 4
                            ♡ 10 8 5
                            ◇ A K 10 8 6
                            ♣ K 2

                    Soloway   Andersen
        East   South   West   North
        Pass   1 NT   2 ♡   2 NT
        3 ♡   4 ◇   5 ♣   5 ◇
        Pass   6 ◇   All Pass

*Asking for better minor

Without the two notrump inquiry available I would have signed off in three clubs; with it we were able to reach an excellent slam. Since I might have been signing off at the three-level, Soloway's free bid of four diamonds had to be based on a very good hand with an excellent fit — probably no wastage in hearts and a fitting honor in clubs. So I felt confident in bidding the game. Once he knew I was willing to be at the five-level, his very good hand got even better. Since he "knew" about the heart shortness and the club suit, he reasoned that six diamonds should have excellent chances.

PART II

LEBENSOHL AFTER
OPPONENTS' WEAK TWO-BIDS

Chapter 8

RESPONDING TO A DOUBLE OF
A WEAK TWO-BID

By this time you should feel fairly comfortable with the basic Lebensohl principles. So let's see how the Lebensohl ideas can be applied to solve problems in other auctions.

A true torture auction for standard bidders starts when the partnership makes a takeout double of an opponent's weak two-bid. A three-level response has such a wide range of strength that it is impossible to bid accurately.

Suppose you pick up:

(a) ♠ 6 3 2   ♡ 9 7   ◊ 10 8 3   ♣ 10 7 6 5 3

and hear:

LHO	Partner	RHO	You
2♠	Double	Pass	?

Now this is a predicament! You can't pass two spades doubled, so you are forced to bid three clubs (with 0 HCP!) and pray partner stops bidding before you need an ambulance.

However, if your hand is:

(b) ♠ 10 5 4   ♡ K 8   ◊ 10 9 4   ♣ K Q 10 8 7,

after the same start, what will you bid? Probably three clubs, hoping that partner will be able to scrape up another bid so that you can show your full strength.

What a difference between these two hands! Yet three clubs is your only plausible action in both cases. With hand (a) you must do something — what else but three clubs? And, with hand (b), you are not strong enough for a jump to four clubs, not to mention that the jump will take you past your most likely game — three no-trump). What else can you bid but three clubs? You consider a slight overbid of three spades, but what will you do when your ever-predictable partner tries the inevitable four hearts instead of the hoped-for three notrump?

Now let's examine the problems from the other side of the table. Assume you have doubled a two spade opening with:

♠ A J   ♡ Q J 4 2   ◇ A Q 9 8   ♣ A J 9

Partner responds with three clubs. If the poor fellow was unlucky enough to be dealt hand (a)

♠ 6 3 2   ♡ 9 7   ◇ 10 7 3   ♣ 10 7 6 5 3,

you'd better pass fast and run for the hills. One move past three clubs is sure to bring on a painful barrage of penalty doubles. But if partner holds our second example hand

♠ 10 5 4   ♡ K 8   ◇ 10 7 4   ♣ K Q 10 8 7,

or even a slightly better hand, three notrump is unbreakable; playing in a part-score will provide a poor result at any form of scoring.

Obviously, both responder and doubler are impaled on the horns of a dilemma in auctions such as this one. Fortunately, our old friend Lebensohl comes to the rescue with a simple but most effective solution.

Once again, though, you have to give up the natural meaning of two notrump — a relatively infrequent response. This is how it works:

**LEBENSOHL AFTER A
TAKEOUT DOUBLE OF A WEAK TWO-BID**

(1) Responder's two notrump forces the doubler to rebid three clubs, enabling responder to sign off in his long suit with a weak hand. (Exactly the same as in Lebensohl after one notrump interference.)

(2) Responder's non-jump suit bid at the three-level is constructive, informing partner that he has some useful values.

Very simple! But what a difference this neat little device makes in the auction. Now responder has two ways to bid three clubs — one weak and one constructive. With hand (a) he starts with two notrump (warning partner that he is weak) and passes the doubler's forced three club rebid. With hand (b) he bids three clubs (constructive), showing some moderate strength. Responder's doubts evaporate into thin air. And the doubler's problems also disappear. After the two notrump response the doubler is happy to get out in three clubs. But after the constructive three club bid he happily carries on to game.

"Useful Values"

Opponent	Partner	Opponent	You
2 ♣	Double	Pass	3 ♣

What is the exact strength shown by the three club call? Rule 2 tells us that responder's simple suit bid at the three level shows some useful values. But exactly what constitutes useful values?

The dividing line between a poor hand and a constructive response is generally considered to be around 7 HCP; responder should use the two notrump relay with 0 up to a poor 7 count and make a constructive change-of-suit call at the three-level with a good 7 HCP up to about a poor 11 count. With a good 11 or more, responder should employ a stronger initial response (i.e., a jump or a cue-bid).

A few examples:

Opponent	Partner	Opponent	You
2 ♠	Double	Pass	?

♠ 10 9   ♡ A J 9 7   ◊ Q 10 9 5   ♣ 9 8 7

Bid 3 Hearts. Constructive. You have 7 HCP — enough to make a progressive move but not enough to force to game. Note that you should choose three hearts, not three diamonds. There's a bonus for bidding and making game, and four hearts is easier than five diamonds. Not only that, but partner is more likely to hold four hearts than four diamonds for his takeout double of two spades.

♠ 5 3   ♡ J 10 8 5   ◊ Q 4 3 2   ♣ 8 6 3

Bid 2 Notrump. Partner must bid three clubs, then you sign off in three hearts. With only 3 HCP you must warn partner that you are weak. Once again, it is better to choose hearts in preference to diamonds, not for the game possibilities, but because, as we mentioned previously, partner is slightly more likely to have four hearts than four diamonds for his takeout double.

♠ 10 8   ♡ A J 10 9   ◊ A Q 10 7   ♣ 10 8 7

Bid 3 Spades. With 11 HCP and two good suits, you are much too strong to allow the auction to die below game. Start with a cue-bid, planning to follow with four hearts.

Note: All cue-bids, two-level bids and jumps retain the same meaning they would have had if you were not using Lebensohl.

The following deal from a recent ACBL NAC fully illustrates the value of the Lebensohl approach after the opponents' weak two-bid. North-South were Kathie Wei and Judi Radin, winners of numerous World, National and Regional championships.

East-West Vulnerable
East Dealer

North
♠ 10 8 2
♡ K
◊ Q 7 6
♣ Q 10 9 6 5 4

West	East
♠ 4 3	♠ K Q J 9 7 5
♡ J 6 5 4 3	♡ Q 8 2
◊ A K 4 3	◊ J 5 2
♣ J 8	♣ 7

South
♠ A 6
♡ A 10 9 7
◊ 10 9 8
♣ A K 3 2

	Wei		Radin
East	South	West	North
2 ♠	Double	Pass	3 ♣*
Pass	3 NT	All Pass	

*Lebensohl, showing useful values

The Lebensohl convention, combined with excellent judgment, showed a substantial gain in this deal. Radin judged well to show some values, upgrading her hand because of the sixth club and the possibly useful singleton. And Wei did very well indeed to carry on to game, evaluating correctly that her controls and excellent club fit were worth stretching a bit. Without Lebensohl to tell her that her partner had a little something, Wei would have been faced with an out-and-out guess.

Very Strong Hands

Occasionally you will make a takeout double of an opponent's weak two-bid with a very powerful hand and hear partner respond two notrump, warning you of extreme weakness. For example:

RHO	You	LHO	Partner
2 ♠	Double	Pass	2 NT
Pass	?		

♠ A 10 ♡ A K Q ◇ A K Q J 8 ♣ 10 9 7

Bid 3 Notrump. Clearly, you want to be in game with this hand no matter how weak partner's hand is. You cannot afford to accept the relay to three clubs because of the high probability that responder has a very poor hand with a club suit and will pass three clubs. So you must take some stronger action. Three notrump is what you expect to make — so bid it.

♠ 10 6 ♡ A K Q 5 ◇ A K Q J 6 ♣ A 10

Bid 3 Spades. Game forcing cue-bid. As in the previous problem, you want to get to game so you can't risk three clubs. But this time you're not so sure where to play because you don't have the opponents' suit stopped. Three spades virtually forces responder to bid three notrump with a spade stopper. If he has no spade stopper, he will bid a suit at the four-level (probably four clubs), and you can try four diamonds, giving him a chance to bid four hearts or five diamonds.

♠ 7 ♡ A K 10 9 ◇ A K 10 8 7 5 ♣ Q 8

Bid 3 Diamonds. Not forcing, but promising extra strength. You don't want partner to pass three clubs, but you are not strong enough to drive to game all by yourself. If responder has anything which looks useful, he will bid again. Otherwise he will pass three diamonds. If, by chance, he tries to sign off in three hearts with

♠ 10 6 2   ♡ Q J 6 5 3   ◊ Q 2   ♣ 7 6 4,

you will bid game.

<h3 style="text-align:center">General Principle:</h3>

If the doubler makes any call other than three clubs after the two notrump relay, he shows extra strength and invites responder to bid a game.

FADS

Look at this auction:

LHO	Partner	RHO	You
2 ♠	Double	Pass	?

If your hand is

♠ Q 3 2   ♡ A Q 9 6   ◊ 9 8 4   ♣ K J 9,

you know you want to be in game, but you aren't sure which one. Partner has not absolutely guaranteed four hearts with his takeout double, nor has he denied a balanced hand with high cards in the spade suit.

Suppose he has doubled two spades with something like:

(a) ♠ J 9   ♡ K J 2   ◊ A 10 6 3   ♣ A Q 7 4

Three notrump is unbreakable, while four hearts, on the 4-3 fit, may be in trouble.

However, if the doubler's hand is:

(b) ♠ 7   ♡ K J 8 7   ◊ A 10 6 3   ♣ A Q 7 4,

three notrump will not be a great success (unless you are the sort of player lucky enough to find both the ace and king of spades on your left). Surely, you would prefer to be in four hearts.

Using standard methods, all you can do is guess. However, Lebensohl can take away the guess. We have already looked at the Lebensohl approach for showing or denying stoppers in the opponents' suit after one notrump interference. This mechanism can easily be adapted for use after the opponents' weak two-bids.

Remember FADS — Fast Auction Denies Stopper? Let's try applying FADS principles to this type of auction with our example hand:

♠ Q 3 2   ♡ A Q 9 6   ◇ 9 8 4   ♣ K J 9

With a spade stopper and strength enough for game, we will start with two notrump, relaying to three clubs, then bid three spades (cue-bid) describing game-forcing values with a stopper and implying four hearts. (Slow auction shows stopper.)

Note: With a stopper in the opponent's suit and no interest in any contract other than three notrump, we would simply bid three notrump and not bother with the cue-bid. Hence, the cue-bid is very similar in function to the Stayman cue-bid after one notrump interference. It is not called Stayman in this sort of auction (and does **not** guarantee a four-card major), but it operates quite similarly. (See page 66.)

If doubler has hand (a), he will, of course, choose three notrump. But, if he holds (b), he has no doubt that three notrump is the wrong contract. After your delayed cue-bid, showing a stopper but suggesting playability elsewhere, he will bid four hearts.

Suppose after the same sequence your hand is a little different:

♠ 10 3 2   ♡ A Q 9 6   ◇ K 9 8   ♣ K J 9

Now you won't bother with the two notrump relay, but will simply make a direct three spade cue-bid, denying a stopper and forcing to game. (Fast auction denies stopper.)

Now, if opener holds either hand (a) or hand (b), he knows you don't belong in three notrump, so he will look for another contact. With hand (a) he will bid four clubs (denying four hearts) and you can try the 4-3 heart fit (which will probably make). With hand (b) he could go directly to four hearts, but he will probably move toward slam knowing you have no spade wastage — six hearts turns out to be quite a good contract.

Of course, you can choose to employ FASS (Fast Auction Shows Stopper) principles after the opponents' weak two-bids if you wish. However, in this situation, I strongly recommend FADS. Since the slow auction employs two notrump as a relay, I find it beneficial that the player who bids two notrump has a stopper. Otherwise, you risk playing three notrump from the wrong side of the table when the doubler has the stopper and the opening lead comes through his stopper rather than up to it. In fact, a third basic rule for Lebensohl after weak two-bids which I find useful is:

> (3) The player who first bids notrump (in non-signoff sequences) promises a stopper.

Generally, this translates to FADS, with one slight modification. An immediate jump to three notrump promises a stopper even though this is a "fast" auction, because it follows Rule 3. Note that we don't need the jump to three notrump as a "fast auction without a stopper." Unlike Lebensohl after notrump interference, we can make a direct cue-bid denying a stopper without guaranteeing four cards in the unbid major(s).

As a final note on responding to takeout doubles of weak two-bids, here's an auction which may cause you some concern:

RHO	You	LHO	Partner
2 ♡	Double	Pass	2 NT*
Pass	3 ♣	Pass	3 ♠

*Lebensohl

Obviously partner is not trying to sign off in three spades. He could have done that with a bid of two spades over your takeout double. Following Rule 3, he promises a heart stopper. And, since he would cue-bid with four spades, he is promising five spades and offering you a choice of games — three notrump or four spades.

Let's briefly review responding to takeout doubles of weak two-bids:

(Both Vulnerable)

LHO	Partner	RHO	You
2 ♠	Double	Pass	?

(1) ♠ 10 8 ♡ K J 9 2 ◊ 8 7 4 ♣ A 6 5 3

(2) ♠ A Q ♡ K 10 8 7 ◊ Q 10 9 6 ♣ J 4 3

(3) ♠ 4 3 2 ♡ J 8 6 ◊ 10 8 7 2 ♣ Q 6 4

(4) ♠ A 8 4 ♡ 6 5 ◊ A K J 9 8 ♣ 10 8 7

(5) ♠ 7 6 4 ♡ A Q 10 8 ◊ 9 7 ♣ K Q 9 5

(6) ♠ Q J 9 8 ♡ 6 5 3 2 ◊ A 4 ♣ K 10 9

(1) **Bid 3 Hearts.** Showing some moderate strength.

(2) **Bid 2 Notrump.** Follow with three spades showing the spade stopper and implying four hearts.

(3) **Bid 2 Notrump.** Lebensohl. Follow with three diamonds to show weakness. This auction does **not** show a spade stopper because you are in a signoff sequence.

(4) **Bid 3 Notrump.** Too good for three diamonds. Three notrump is what you expect to make, so bid it. Don't fool around with a cue-bid or two notrump sequence — you may find yourself in four hearts!

(5) **Bid 3 Spades.** Denies a stopper and implies four hearts. Alternatively, simply bid four hearts since that is your most likely game.

(6) **Pass and take your plus score.** With 10 HCP and poor hearts, you have no guarantee of a game. But it's near certain that you will beat two spades.

Chapter 9

RESPONDING TO
TWO NOTRUMP OVERCALLS

Consider the following sequence:

LHO	Partner	RHO
2 ♡	2 NT	Pass

Although this auction occurs frequently, it can cause an inexperienced partnership enormous difficulty. Strictly speaking, this auction has nothing to do with Lebensohl *per se*. However, I'm going to cover it here because your arsenal against the opponents' weak two-bids is not complete without a thorough understanding of how your partnership handles a two notrump overcall.

Most of you probably already play that the two notrump overcall shows about a strong notrump (15-18 HCP), which is what I advocate. But then what? Does your partnership know how to proceed after the overcall with these hands?

LHO	Partner	RHO	You
2 ♡	2 NT	Pass	?

(a) ♠ A Q 8 7 5   ♡ Q 6   ◊ 4 2   ♣ Q 10 8 7

How do you tell partner that you might play this hand in four spades, but that three notrump is okay if he doesn't have a spade fit?

(b) ♠ K Q 9 8   ♡ A 9 7   ◊ 8 6 3 2   ♣ 5 3

You can probably make three notrump, but wouldn't you prefer to be in four spades if partner has four, especially if he also holds a weak club suit?

(c) ♠ J 9 8 6 5 2   ♡ 4   ◊ J 9 7 3   ♣ 10 6

You want to play three spades — not four! But will your partner pass your three spade call?

(d) ♠ A J 9 8 6 3 2   ♡ K 3   ◇ A 10 8   ♣ 2

You have definite slam possibilities if partner has a spade honor. You'd like to bid three spades and then investigate, but what if partner passes three spades!

(e) ♠ K Q 2   ♡ 2   ◇ A 9 8 4 3   ♣ K 10 9 7

You certainly have the strength to raise to three notrump, but if partner's heart stopper is shaky, or if he has only one stopper and has to give up the lead to establish your diamond suit, you may wish you had looked for a better spot. You could easily be cold for five of either minor (or even six!), while you are going down in three notrump. Suppose partner has overcalled two notrump with

♠ A J   ♡ A 6 5   ◇ Q 10 7 6 2   ♣ A J 2

You need luck to make three notrump, while six diamonds is a virtual claim! But how are you supposed to bid it? And is three diamonds even forcing?

Do these problems sound familiar? They should; you see them every day at the table. Perhaps you've noticed we've already solved many similar dilemmas in earlier chapters with Lebensohl. But Lebensohl won't help us now because partner has already bid two notrump, the anchor bid in the Lebensohl structure.

Actually these problems are not at all difficult if you adopt the following approach:

AFTER A NATURAL TWO NOTRUMP OVERCALL

(1) Three clubs is Stayman.

(2) Jacoby transfers are used, at least for the majors, but preferably for all four suits.

(3) A transfer to the opponents' suit shows shortness in that suit, game-forcing values and no four-card major.

Let's see how well Stayman and Jacoby work with our problem hands above:

LHO	Partner	RHO	You
2 ♡	2 NT	Pass	?

(a) ♠ A Q 8 7 5   ♡ Q 6   ◊ 4 2   ♣ Q 10 8 7

Bid 3 Hearts, transferring to three spades. Follow with three notrump to give partner a choice of games.

(b) ♠ K Q 9 8   ♡ A 9 7   ◊ 8 6 3 2   ♣ 5 3

Bid 3 Clubs. Stayman. If partner shows four spades, raise to four spades — probably safer than three notrump.

(c) ♠ J 9 8 6 5 2   ♡ 4   ◊ J 9 7 3   ♣ 10 6

Bid 3 Hearts, transferring to three spades. Then pass.

(d) ♠ A J 9 8 6 3 2   ♡ K 3   ◊ A 10 8   ♣ 2

Bid 3 Hearts, transferring to three spades. Follow with whatever bid conveys slam interest in your partnership (four clubs, four diamonds, four hearts, four notrump, five clubs, etc.).

(e) ♠ K Q 2   ♡ 2   ◊ A 9 8 4 3   ♣ K 10 9 7

Bid 3 Diamonds, transferring to three hearts and follow with three notrump. This sequence tells partner that you have a normal raise to three notrump with shortness in hearts. If he doesn't think three notrump will make opposite a singleton heart, he won't pass.

Did you notice how easily all your former problems disappeared? Try these hands yourself:

LHO	Partner	RHO	You
2 ♠	2 NT	Pass	?

(1) ♠ 8 4 3   ♡ K Q 9 5 3 2   ◊ 6 3   ♣ 8 7

(2) ♠ A 9 5   ♡ K Q 9 7   ◊ 8 7   ♣ 8 7 6 2

(3) ♠ 6 3   ♡ K 9 5 4   ◊ 8 6 5   ♣ Q 8 4 2

(4) ♠ 8   ♡ A Q 7 5   ◊ K 7 5 4   ♣ 9 7 4 2

(5) ♠ 3   ♡ K Q 8 6 4 3   ◊ A Q J 7 2   ♣ 9

(1) Bid 3 Diamonds. Transfer to three hearts. Pass partner's forced rebid.

(2) **Bid 3 Clubs.** (Stayman). If opener shows four hearts, raise to four hearts; otherwise bid three notrump.

(3) **Pass.** Not good enough for Stayman — you have nowhere to go if partner rebids three diamonds denying four hearts.

(4) **Bid 3 Clubs.** (Stayman). Do **not** bid three hearts. This time you have four hearts and the transfer to the opponents' suit denies a four-card major.

(5) **Bid 3 Diamonds.** Transfer to three hearts. Follow with four diamonds, getting both of your suits in below four hearts. (Four diamonds is forcing.)

As you no doubt know from your experience with transfers over one notrump, your initial minor suit bids are no longer natural. So what do you do with

(a) ♠ 5 ♡ A 4 3 ◊ K Q 10 8 7 6 2 ♣ Q 9, or

(b) ♠ 8 7 ♡ 2 ◊ 6 5 ♣ J 10 8 7 6 5 3 2,

after

LHO	Partner	RHO	
2 ♡	2 NT	Pass	?

There are two possible answers:

(1) Don't bid with these hands.

(2) Play four-suit transfers.

Obviously, I choose the second since I'm not enchanted with hands I can't bid!

Here's how four-suit transfers work after a two notrump overcall of a weak two-bid. (A transfer to the opponent's suit is forcing, denying a stopper.)

- Three clubs is Stayman.
- Three diamonds transfers to three hearts.
- Three hearts transfers to three spades.
- Three spades transfers to four clubs.
- Four clubs (jump) transfers to four diamonds.

This may seem a little strange at first, but it's very simple to handle once you get used to it. If you are already using transfers, you probably have no meaning for the three spade call anyway. So the only new bid is the jump to four clubs as a transfer to diamonds.

Let's go back to those two problem hands:

(a) ♠ 5 ♡ A 4 3 ◇ K Q 10 8 7 6 2 ♣ Q 9

Bid 4 Clubs, transferring to four diamonds. Follow with a cue-bid of four hearts to make a slam try. You cannot have four hearts because you didn't use Stayman!

(b) ♠ 8 7 ♡ 2 ◇ 6 5 ♣ J 10 8 7 6 5 3 2

Bid 3 Spades, transferring to four clubs. You probably won't make it, but it must be a better contract than two notrump; at least you can take some trump tricks. If you get lucky, you might make ten or even eleven tricks if partner has the right cards.

QUIZ ON PART II

This quiz is designed to challenge your new skills with Lebensohl. Many of the problems are difficult and the suggested solution may not be clearcut.

After

LHO	Partner	RHO	You
2 ♡	Double	Pass	?

What do you bid with each of these hands?

(1) ♠ Q 9 7 3   ♡ A 4   ◇ 7 6 3   ♣ 10 4 3 2

(2) ♠ J 10 9 7 3   ♡ A 4   ◇ K J 9   ♣ 4 3 2

(3) ♠ Q 10 8 2   ♡ A 10 8   ◇ K Q 4 2   ♣ Q 7

(4) ♠ A Q 4 3   ♡ 4 3 2   ◇ Q J 10   ♣ K 9 8

(5) ♠ A Q 3   ♡ 4 3   ◇ Q J 10 8   ♣ Q J 10 4

(6) ♠ 7 6 3   ♡ Q 3 2   ◇ K J 10 6   ♣ Q 10 9

(7) ♠ A 2   ♡ 6 5 3   ◇ 9 8 5 4 2   ♣ 7 6 5

(8) ♠ J 6 5 3 2   ♡ K 10 9   ◇ A Q 7   ♣ 6 3

Answers

(1) **Bid 2 Spades.** You have less than game invitational values.

(2) **Bid 3 Spades.** Invitational.

(3) **Bid 2 Notrump.** Follow with three hearts (cue-bid), showing a heart stopper and forcing to game.

(4) **Bid 3 Hearts.** Game-forcing cue-bid with no heart stopper.

(5) **Bid 3 Hearts.** Game-forcing cue-bid. Does not promise four spades.

(6) **Bid 3 Diamonds.** Showing some useful values.

(7) **Bid 2 Notrump.** Lebensohl. Follow with three diamonds, signoff.

(8) **Bid 2 Notrump.** Follow with three spades (forcing). Shows a heart stopper and five spades and gives partner a choice of games.

After

LHO	Partner	RHO	You
2 ♠	Double	Pass	?

What do you do with

(9) ♠ K J 10   ♡ Q 10 9 5   ◇ A 6 3   ♣ K 10 7

(10) ♠ 7 3 2   ♡ 4   ◇ K 5 3   ♣ 10 9 8 6 4 3

(11) ♠ 8 6   ♡ 4 2   ◇ A Q 10 9 7 2   ♣ K Q 8

(12) ♠ 9 7   ♡ A 10 8 7 6   ◇ 8   ♣ Q J 10 8 2

(13) ♠ A Q   ♡ K J 10 7   ◇ 10 7 5   ♣ 10 9 8 6

(14) ♠ 6   ♡ A   ◇ K Q 10 9 8 4   ♣ 8 7 5 3 2

Answers

(9) **Bid 2 Notrump.** Follow with three spades (cue-bid). Shows spade stopper and implies four hearts. Too good for three hearts constructive.

(10) **Bid 2 Notrump.** Pass partner's three clubs. This is a pretty good hand for a sign-off, but you can't push with only 3 HCP, even with a six-card suit and a singleton. If there is a chance of game partner will bid more than three clubs.

(11) **Bid 4 Diamonds.** Highly invitational. A very difficult hand — borderline between an invitational four diamonds and the game-forcing three spades (cue-bid). It will not be possible to take eleven tricks opposite most minimum take-out doubles and we may even go down at the four-level, so it's the right time to be somewhat conservative. Three spades would be okay if partner would promise not to bid four hearts!

(12) **Bid 4 Hearts.** Sign-off. Based on shape, not high cards. With the high card strength to force to game you should start with a cue-bid.

(13) **Bid 2 Notrump.** Follow with three spades (cue-bid). A slight overbid, but the hand justifies the stretch with two stoppers and good spots.

(14) **Bid 5 Diamonds.** Sign-off. Only 9 HCP, but the distribution should be sufficient to produce game.

After

RHO	You	LHO	Partner
2 ♠	Double	Pass	3 ♣
Pass	?		

What is your rebid with

(15) ♠ 9 7   ♡ K Q J 6   ◇ A 10 8 4   ♣ K J 9

(16) ♠ 10   ♡ A Q 10 7   ◇ K Q J 5   ♣ K Q 4 3

(17) ♠ K 4   ♡ A J 10 3   ◇ A 7 5 3   ♣ K Q 5

Answers

(15) **Pass.** Partner has some values, but he has a maximum of 10 HCP. There is no game in sight.

(16) **Bid 3 Spades.** Partner's 7 to 10 HCP make your hand good enough to move toward game. If partner rebids three notrump or four clubs you will pass. If he does anything else you will bid game.

(17) **Bid 3 Notrump.** You may not make it, but it will often be cold. Partner may have

♠ 5 3   ♡ 8 7 5   ◇ K 8 4   ♣ A J 9 6 4,

and three notrump is virtually unbeatable while no other game has much play.

After

LHO	Partner	RHO	You
2 ♠	2 NT*	Pass	?

*15-18 HCP

What action do you take with

(18) ♠ 10 9 7   ♡ K 10 9 7 5   ◊ K Q 9   ♣ 8 6

(19) ♠ 7   ♡ K 8 4   ◊ A K J 10 8   ♣ 9 8 4 2

(20) ♠ Q 7 6 3   ♡ A 9 8 3 2   ◊ K 4   ♣ 7 3

(21) ♠ A 6   ♡ 9 7 6 4 2   ◊ K 5 2   ♣ Q J 9

(22) ♠ 7 5 4   ♡ A 9 4 3 2   ◊ 9 6 4   ♣ 9 7

(23) ♠ 8   ♡ Q 8 5 4   ◊ J 7 6 3   ♣ 10 9 8 6

(24) ♠ 7 5   ♡ 9 4 3   ◊ Q 10 8 7 5 4 2   ♣ 7

(25) ♠ J 3   ♡ Q 10 8   ◊ 7 4   ♣ K Q J 10 5 3

Answers

(18) **Bid 3 Diamonds.** Transfer to three hearts. Follow with three notrump. A slight overbid, but it usually pays to overbid rather than underbid when you have no invitation available. Also, your side has a lot of information about the opponents' hands to help in the play.

(19) **Bid 3 Notrump.** *Not* three hearts. Partner has a spade stopper, and with your good suit you expect him to make three notrump despite your singleton spade. There is no point in asking him to make a decision which you can make yourself.

(20) **Bid 3 Notrump.** *Not* three diamonds. You have a bad heart suit and too many spades to expect four hearts to play well.

(21) **Bid 3 Notrump.** *Not* three diamonds. Your hearts are too porous to consider game in that suit. And you have help in all the other suits.

(22) **Pass.** Partner has not promised a heart fit, so don't put him in what might be a bad part-score. Two notrump is the least of evils.

(23) **Pass.** Not strong enough for Stayman — you have nowhere to go over partner's possible three diamond rebid.

(24) **Bid 4 Clubs.** Transferring to four diamonds. Then pass.

(25) **Bid 3 Notrump.** You expect to make three notrump and you have no slam interest, so don't foul up the auction with a transfer to clubs.

PART III

LEBENSOHL
AFTER A REVERSE

Chapter 10
RESPONDING TO A REVERSE

The vast majority of bridge players treat a reverse by opener as a one-round force showing extra strength. Responder cannot pass. For example, in the sequence

Opener	Responder
1 ◇	1 ♠
2 ♡	?

two hearts is a reverse; responder must bid again.

Most partnerships agree that the strength required for a reverse starts with a lower range of an exceptional 16 HCP, but it is unlimited, and often contains the same strength as that required for a strong jump-shift. But there is little, if any, agreement about what responder is supposed to do next.

Consider responder's choice of rebids holding these hands:

(a)   ♠ J 5 4 2   ♡ 6 3   ◇ Q 6 4 3   ♣ Q J 8

(b)   ♠ A Q J 10   ♡ 10 9 7   ◇ K J 10 6   ♣ A 10

With hand (a) all he wants to do is to warn partner that he has a very poor hand. Unless opener has an exceptional reverse, he wants to stop in three diamonds. However, with hand (b) he'd like to bid three diamonds to set the trump suit and then explore for a likely slam. Obviously he cannot bid three diamonds with both hands unless opener plays bridge with a crystal ball.

Or, what about

(c)   ♠ J 10 9 6 4 3   ♡ 8 7   ◇ J 6   ♣ Q J 2

(d)   ♠ A 10 8 7 6 2   ♡ A 9   ◇ 10 9   ♣ Q 6 3

With hand (c) responder would like to get out in two spades; if partner bids again it will not bring him any joy. However, with hand (d) he'd like to rebid two spades on the way to game, since a 6-2 spade fit might produce the best game. But if opener passes this time, the result will be a calamity.

If your current approach is to bid two spades holding either hand (c) or (d) (with a desperate prayer in your heart that opener guesses right), you have probably scored up + 230 and − 800 often enough that you are anxious for some improvement in your methods.

Several questions arise after the reverse:

- Is the reverse completely game-forcing?
- If not, must opener always bid again?
- What strength do responder's rebids show?
- Which bids are forcing? And which are game-forcing?
- How does responder say that he is very weak and would like to get out below game?
- How does he confirm a fit for one of opener's suits to begin an investigation for slam?

Clearly, bidding after a reverse is a murky area full of ambiguities. Happily, there is a simple panacea for all of this confusion. The Lebensohl principles we've been discussing after one notrump interference and weak two-bids can easily be applied to the reverse auction. As with all other applications of Lebensohl, all that is required is to give up the natural meaning of a two notrump rebid by responder. The mechanics are simply:

LEBENSOHL AFTER A REVERSE

(1) After a reverse, two notrump by responder is artificial and forces opener to rebid three clubs, enabling responder to sign off at the three-level.*

(2) Any response other than two notrump is natural, constructive and game-forcing.

*Note: Since opener is unlimited he can, and will, bid more than three clubs when he is too good to allow responder to pass three clubs.

This simple structure provides a straightforward answer for responder's dilemmas. He gets out below game by starting with the artificial Lebensohl two notrump. All other calls are natural and force to game. The auction is allowed to develop naturally, with both opener and responder secure in the knowledge that partner will not pass below game. Even slam investigation becomes a simple matter once the partnership is safely in a game-forcing auction.

The Constructive Response

The basic rules for Lebensohl after opener's reverse say that any rebid other than two notrump is constructive. But you may wonder exactly what is meant by "constructive." Just what strength does a constructive response show?

The answer is obvious. If responder has enough strength to get to at least a game opposite opener's minimum reverse, his hand qualifies for a constructive response. An easy way to think of the constructive, or progressive, response is "game-forcing values." There is no need for an upper limit on a constructive response since it is forcing at least to game.

Using the methods outlined above, let's find out how responder should handle our problem examples.

Opener	Responder
1 ◇	1 ♠
2 ♡	?

(a) ♠ J 5 4 2   ♡ 6 3   ◇ Q 6 4 3   ♣ Q J 8

(b) ♠ A Q J 10   ♡ 10 9 7   ◇ K J 10 6   ♣ A 10

(c) ♠ J 10 9 6 4 3   ♡ 8 7   ◇ J 6   ♣ Q J 2

(d) ♠ A 10 8 7 6 2   ♡ A 9   ◇ 10 9   ♣ Q 6 3

(a) **Bid 2 Notrump.** Lebensohl. A relay to three clubs, allowing you to sign off in three diamonds.

(b) **Bid 3 Diamonds.** Constructive and game-forcing. Sets the trump suit and paves the way for slam investigation.

(c) **Bid 2 Notrump.** Lebensohl. Follow with three spades, signoff. (You can't get out in two spades.)

(d) **Bid 2 Spades.** Game-forcing.

Try these hands. What action would you take as responder after partner's reverse?

Opener	Responder
1 ♣	1 ♠
2 ♡	?

(1) ♠ J 9 6 5 3　♡ J 10　◇ Q 8 5　♣ Q 7 6

(2) ♠ K Q 10 5 4　♡ Q 9 8 2　◇ 9　♣ Q 10 4

(3) ♠ A J 5 3 2　♡ K 3　◇ 7 4　♣ J 8 3 2

(4) ♠ A Q J 9 6　♡ Q 8 4　◇ 5 3　♣ J 6 2

(5) ♠ A Q 10 8　♡ 8 5　◇ K Q 9 2　♣ 7 6 3

(1) **Bid 2 Notrump.** Lebensohl. Forces opener to rebid three clubs which you intend to pass. Don't forget that you cannot show a three club preference immediately. That would promise good club support and game-forcing values.

(2) **Bid 3 Hearts.** Constructive, game-forcing. Promises at least four-card heart support.

(3) **Bid 3 Clubs.** Game-forcing values with good club fit.

(4) **Bid 2 Spades.** Constructive, game-forcing. It is fine to rebid a good five-card major suit after opener's reverse; king doubleton in opener's hand would certainly be adequate trump support.

(5) **Bid 2 Notrump.** Lebensohl, relaying to three clubs. Ostensibly a signoff, but when you follow with three notrump, partner will know you hold a natural game-forcing two notrump.

The Reverse to Two Diamonds
(The Exception to the Rule)

As a rule, when one hand is very strong while the opposite hand is weak, it is preferable for the strong hand to become declarer in the final contract because of the value of the opening lead coming up to any possible tenaces. In addition, if the strong hand is on the table, most of the partnership's resources are revealed to the opponents and they can defend almost double dummy.

If opener has the minors and is strong enough to reverse, notrump is often likely to become the final contract. And the least likely suit to play in is the one that has not yet been bid — the "fourth suit" — the unbid major.

With this thought in mind, when opener has bid both minors, the fourth suit can be used (instead of two notrump), to announce a weak hand and request that opener rebid three clubs. Then two notrump by responder becomes a natural game-force. Examine the two sequences below:

Opener	Responder		Opener	Responder
1 ♣	1 ♡	or	1 ♣	1 ♠
2 ♢	2 ♠		2 ♢	2 ♡

These are the only two reverse auctions where the bid of the fourth suit replaces the two notrump bid. In each auction responder's second bid asks opener to rebid three clubs so that responder can get out below game. Opener can then choose to rebid notrump when he thinks it may play better from his side of the table.

You cannot use this maneuver so easily in the two other reverse sequences,

Opener	Responder		Opener	Responder
1 ♢	1 ♠	or	1 ♣	1 ♠
2 ♡			2 ♡	

because the fourth suit is at the three-level, forcing the auction too high for a convenient signoff.

You can, of course, use Lebensohl after reverses without this refinement. However, I highly recommend that you adopt it. It's worth the slight extra memory work involved to insure that you don't "wrong-side" the final contract. I would go so far as to make another basic rule for Lebensohl in reverse auctions:

**LEBENSOHL AFTER A REVERSE
TO TWO DIAMONDS**

(3) After a reverse to two diamonds, responder uses the fourth suit (instead of two notrump) to show weakness. Opener is forced to rebid three clubs. (Responder's two notrump becomes a natural force.)

What rebid would you make as responder with these hands?

Opener	Responder
1 ♣	1 ♡
2 ♦	?

(1) ♠ 6 4 3   ♡ K 9 6 3 2   ♦ 10 8 4 2   ♣ Q

(2) ♠ A 4   ♡ A 9 6 5   ♦ 10 3 2   ♣ K J 8 4

(3) ♠ A J 5   ♡ K 7 5 4   ♦ Q 9 6   ♣ 8 6 3

(4) ♠ 8 2   ♡ A Q 10 9 3   ♦ K 6 2   ♣ 4 3 2

(5) ♠ 7 5 2   ♡ Q 10 8 7 6 4   ♦ Q 6   ♣ 8 7

(1) **Bid 2 Spades.** Fourth suit. Forces opener to rebid three clubs so that you can sign off in three diamonds. Remember that the fourth suit replaces two notrump to show weakness when opener has reversed to two diamonds. (If opener rebids two notrump instead of three clubs, responder still signs off in three diamonds.)

(2) **Bid 3 Clubs.** Setting the trump suit. A small slam is a virtual certainty and there are even possibilities of a grand. Create a force so that you can probe for the proper level. Remember that three clubs is constructive, unlimited and 100% forcing.

(3) **Bid 2 Notrump.** Natural, constructive and game-forcing.

(4) **Bid 2 Hearts.** Natural, constructive and game-forcing.

(5) **Bid 2 Spades.** Not two hearts. The fourth suit forces opener to rebid three clubs so you can sign off in three hearts; two hearts would be game forcing.

Opener's Very Strong Reverses

Suppose you pick up as dealer

(a) ♠ 8 5   ♡ A Q   ♦ K J 10 6   ♣ A Q 10 8 4, or

(b) ♠ A 8   ♡ 10   ♦ A Q 10 4   ♣ K Q J 10 3 2

and the auction unfolds along these lines:

Opener	Responder
1 ♣	1 ♠
2 ♦	2 ♡

Responder's two hearts is the artificial fourth suit bid and replaces two notrump as the start of a signoff sequence after your two diamond rebid. With either of these hands, you are happy to honor partner's request to rebid three clubs. If he passes, you can be confident that you haven't missed anything. But suppose your hand is much better:

(c) ♠ 8 5   ♡ A Q   ◇ A K J 10   ♣ A K Q 10 8

(d) ♠ 9   ♡ A   ◇ A K 8 7 6   ♣ K J 10 8 5 3

(e) ♠ 9   ♡ A   ◇ K Q J 9 8   ♣ K Q J 10 9 8

Now what do you do? With any of these "rocks" you are well aware of the danger of missing a game (and maybe even a slam) if responder passes three clubs.

The solution is the same one that we used in the similar situation when the opponents made a weak two-bid and the takeout doubler was considerably over-strength. Don't rebid three clubs! If you do, you have given responder license to pass. When you don't want to hear him pass, find another call. The general principle developed to compete against weak two bids has a useful application in the reverse auction as well:

If the reverser makes any call other than three clubs after the artificial signoff, he shows extra strength and invites responder to bid game.

(c) **Bid 3 Notrump.** You expect to make a game opposite almost anything, and you have the unbid suit doubly stopped. (Remember that hearts have not really been bid — two hearts was artificial. Therefore, you need a heart stopper to bid notrump.)

(d) **Bid 3 Diamonds.** Showing a fifth diamond as well as game interest opposite partner's potential signoff.

(e) **Bid 4 Diamonds.** You can make a game opposite the diamond queen. Don't let partner pass unless he has a totally worthless hand.

The following deal clearly illustrates the enormous value of the Lebensohl signoff auction. When it came up during a morning knockout match at a recent NAC, I was playing with one of my favorite partners, many time world champion Paul Soloway. His usual excellent judgment, combined with our methods, produced a nice swing in our favor.

North-South Vulnerable
North Dealer

North
♠ K Q 9 4 2
♡ 7 4 3 2
◇ 5 3 2
♣ 4

West
♠ 10 7 6
♡ Q 9 5
◇ K Q 10 8
♣ J 5 2

East
♠ J 8 5
♡ J 6
◇ A J 9 7 4
♣ Q 9 3

South
♠ A 3
♡ A K 10 8
◇ 6
♣ A K 10 8 7 6

Anderson		Soloway	
North	East	South	West
Pass	Pass	1 ♣	Pass
1 ♠	Pass	2 ♡	Pass
2 NT*	Pass	3 ♣	Pass
3 ♡	Pass	4 ♡	Pass
Pass	Pass		

*Lebensohl. Requests three clubs en route to signoff.

Most pairs would either play a part score or get too high on this deal. Our opponents reached six hearts and went down after a diamond lead. If North raises two hearts to three, it would take the entire United States Army to stop South from bidding a slam. However, armed with the information given by the Lebensohl signoff sequence, Soloway knew we did not have a slam. He reluctantly, but wisely, signed off in four hearts and was rewarded with a gain of 13 MPs for his fine judgment.

Before we move on to still more difficult problems, let's review what we've learned about Lebensohl after a reverse.

Opener	Responder
1 ♣	1 ♠
2 ♡	?

What do you rebid with the following hands?

(1) ♠ K Q 8 5 3　♡ 6 5 4　◇ 9 5　♣ 4 3 2

(2) ♠ Q 8 6 5 4　♡ J 5 4 2　◇ K 6　♣ 9 5

(3) ♠ 5 4 3 2　♡ A 10 9　◇ 10 3　♣ A 8 7 3

(4) ♠ K 10 8 7 6 4 3　♡ 9 6　◇ J 9　♣ 10 2

(1) **Bid 2 Notrump.** Lebensohl. Pass opener's three club rebid.

(2) **Bid 2 Notrump.** Follow with three hearts, signoff. Don't forget that a direct raise to three hearts is constructive.

(3) **Bid 3 Clubs.** Natural game-force.

(4) **Bid 2 Notrump.** Relay to three clubs. Follow with three spades, signoff. Remember that a rebid of two spades after opener's two hearts creates a game-force.

Opener	Responder
1 ♣	1 ♡
2 ◇	?

What call should responder make with:

(5) ♠ A 4　♡ K 10 9 8 6 5 3　◇ 6 4　♣ 10 3

(6) ♠ 6 4　♡ A 8 7 6 5　◇ 7 4 3　♣ Q 5 2

(5) **Bid 2 Hearts.** Natural, game-force.

(6) **Bid 2 Spades.** Fourth suit. Artificial relay to three clubs for sign-off purposes. Pass three clubs.

Opener	Responder
1 ♣	1 ♠
2 ♡	2 NT

What should opener rebid with:

(7) ♠ K J   ♡ A 9 5 4   ◇ A 7   ♣ K Q 10 7 6

(8) ♠ A J 10   ♡ K Q J 5   ◇ 5   ♣ A Q J 9 7

(9) ♠ —   ♡ Q 10 8 7 6   ◇ A K   ♣ K Q J 10 6 4

(10) ♠ Q   ♡ A Q J 6   ◇ K Q J   ♣ A Q J 10 9

(7) **Bid 3 Clubs.** Two notrump asked you to rebid three clubs. If responder passes you are happy to play there.

(8) **Bid 3 Spades.** Two notrump asked you to rebid three clubs, but you may miss a game if you do so. Show spade support now so that responder will bid a game if he can.

(9) **Bid 3 Hearts.** You can't give up easily with so many playing tricks. Responder will strain to bid a game when you fail to rebid the normal three clubs.

(10) **Bid 3 Notrump.** You expect to make it opposite most hands that can respond at the one-level, so don't give partner a chance to pass below game.

The Tough Hands

So far most of the reverse auctions we've dealt with have been quite straightforward. The basic rules have led us to the best solution fairly routinely. Unfortunately, not every hand fits neatly into the rules. For example, what should responder do with these nightmares?

Opener	Responder
1 ♣	1 ♡
2 ◇	?

(Both Vulnerable)

♠ Q 5 4 3 2   ♡ Q J 9 8 4 2   ◇ J   ♣ 8

Bid 2 Spades. What a mess! Why didn't I pass one club? It will take Houdini to get us out of this trap. My only hope is to bid the artificial fourth suit (start of a signoff) and then retreat to three hearts.

Opener	Responder
1 ◇	1 ♠
2 ♡	?

♠ A Q 10 8   ♡ K J   ◇ 9 8 6   ♣ K J 8 2

Bid 3 Notrump. With values to invite a slam you must take some aggressive action. We have already seen that responder can "sign off" with game-forcing balanced hands by starting with the artificial Lebensohl two notrump, and then correcting to three notrump over opener's three club rebid. But there must be an upper limit to this sequence so that responder can make a slam move with stronger balanced hands like this one. I suggest about 12 to 13 HCP as a maximum for the Lebensohl sequence. Responder should jump to three notrump with a good looking 13 up to about 15. (With more than 15 HCP, responder has more than just slam "interest" and should, therefore, not make a passable bid. It is a better course with very strong balanced hands to make a simple forcing bid and let opener complete his description.)

NOTE: If your partnership style is to use the principle of "fast arrival," you may wish to reverse the procedure suggested above. Many of you have probably agreed that in auctions where a simple response is forcing, a jump to game is a signoff. This allows you to stay low for slam investigation. If this is your general approach, consistency dictates that you may want to jump to three notrump with, say, 8 to 11 HCP and go slowly with better hands. In this case

Opener	Responder
1 ♣	1 ♠
2 ♡	2 NT
3 ♣	3 NT

would show mild slam interest with up to about 14 to 15 balanced points.

Reverses After a One Notrump Response

Until now we've been looking at opener's reverses after a one-of-a-suit response. But what about

Opener	Responder
1 ♣	1 NT
2 ◇	

or

Opener	Responder
1 ♡	1 NT
2 ♠	

Can we use Lebensohl here?

Yes and no. It can get quite complicated. We'll deal with this in the last chapter when we cover some advanced applications of the Lebensohl ideas. For the time being I would say no — not until you've mastered the basics of Lebensohl and understand them thoroughly. But forewarned is forearmed. If you're still game, go ahead.

QUIZ ON PART III

This quiz has been designed to challenge your new skills with Lebensohl after opener's reverse. Many of the hands are difficult and some of the suggested solutions may not be all that obvious.

After this start:

Opener	Responder
1 ◇	1 ♠
2 ♡	?

What call should responder make with each of these hands?

(1) ♠ K J 6 5   ♡ 10 8 6   ◇ Q 9 4   ♣ J 8 2

(2) ♠ Q J 8 3   ♡ J 7   ◇ 10   ♣ J 10 9 6 4 2

(3) ♠ J 10 9 4 3 2   ♡ K 6   ◇ A 6   ♣ 10 5 3

(4) ♠ A 7 6 4   ♡ K Q 10 8   ◇ Q 3   ♣ J 10 6

(5) ♠ A K 8 6 5 3   ♡ K Q 8 7 2   ◇ 9   ♣ 5

(6) ♠ K 10 9 8 3 2   ♡ 7 6   ◇ 9   ♣ 10 8 7 3

(7) ♠ 9 8 5 4 3   ♡ J 9 6 4   ◇ 7 2   ♣ A J

(8) ♠ A 8 7 5 4   ♡ Q   ◇ K Q J 7 6   ♣ 9 8

(9) ♠ Q J 10 6 2   ♡ 5 3   ◇ 8   ♣ Q 10 7 4 2

Answers

(1) **Bid 2 Notrump.** Lebensohl, forcing opener to rebid three clubs. Follow with a signoff in three diamonds.

(2) **Bid 2 Notrump.** Planning to pass opener's forced three club rebid.

(3) **Bid 2 Spades.** Natural. Constructive game-force.

(4) **Bid 3 Hearts.** Forcing to game. Once the force is established and the heart fit has been revealed you plan to investigate the possibilities of slam.

(5) **Bid 4 Notrump.** Blackwood. Don't bid three hearts. You have a clear objective. You need two aces to make six hearts and three to make seven hearts. Don't get tangled up in a conventional auction just because you have it available. Suppose you bid three hearts and opener rebids three notrump — now how do you ask for aces?

(6) **Bid 2 Notrump. Not** two spades, which would be a game-force. You responded because of your good spades and singleton diamond, but the worst has happened. Do the best you can with a signoff in three spades. Maybe you'll make it.

(7) **Bid 2 Notrump.** Relay to three clubs. Then sign off in three hearts.

(8) **Bid 4 Diamonds.** You have a great hand for opener — tell him! Of course, three diamonds would be forcing, but it doesn't do justice to your hand. Four diamonds describes the nature of this hand — great hand with great diamonds.

(9) **Bid 2 Notrump.** Start of a signoff — **not** two spades which would be game-forcing. This is a disaster-prone hand, but you may survive. If opener rebids three clubs, pass and hope for the best. Or he may rebid three diamonds, promising six, and you can pass. Best of all, he may show spade support! The important point is, don't panic!

Suppose the auction has been:

Opener	Responder
1 ♣	1 ♡
2 ◇	?

What should responder do now with:

(10) ♠ 5   ♡ 7 6 4 3   ◇ A 10 8   ♣ J 9 8 5 4

(11) ♠ A 5   ♡ 8 6 5 4 3 2   ◇ 9 6 4   ♣ Q 8

(12) ♠ A J 10 9   ♡ K Q 7 6   ◇ 8 5 4   ♣ 4 2

(13) ♠ 7 5 3   ♡ Q 10 8 6   ◇ A J 6 2   ♣ Q 3

(14) ♠ K 4   ♡ Q J 6 4   ◇ 5 4 2   ♣ J 9 8 6

(15) ♠ A 9 8 6 5   ♡ J 10 8 7 5 3   ◇ 6   ♣ 2

(16) ♠ Q 9 8 6   ♡ A Q J 8   ◇ K 10   ♣ Q 7 5

(17) ♠ Q 8 7 6   ♡ 10 7 6 5 4 2   ◇ J   ♣ Q J

(18) ♠ A Q 10 9 3   ♡ K Q 10 9 8 6   ◇ 7   ♣ 2

Answers

(10) **Bid 3 Clubs.** Game-force. You have only 5 HCP, but your hand is much too valuable as dummy in a club contract to start a signoff sequence. Remember that partner has a strong hand with nine or ten cards in the minors.

(11) **Bid 2 Spades.** Fourth suit. Pass three clubs or follow with three diamonds, signoff — a guess at best, but it is likely that the hand will play better in one of partner's good suits than in your anemic heart suit.

(12) **Bid 2 Notrump.** *Not* two spades. Two spades would be an artificial start of a signoff sequence, not a natural call, so it is a waste of time and will mislead partner. Two notrump is natural and game-forcing, reflecting just what you have.

(13) **Bid 3 Diamonds.** Natural game-force.

(14) **Bid 2 Spades.** Fourth suit, intending to pass opener's three club rebid. This is a close decision — it could be right to force to game. If opener should happen to rebid two notrump instead of three clubs, indicating game interest opposite a signoff, raise him to three notrump. Three clubs (or three diamonds or three hearts, for that matter) would still be a signoff over opener's two notrump.

(15) **Bid 2 Spades.** Artificial fourth suit bid. Follow with three hearts, signoff. Forget spades; your hand is not good enough, and opener is unlikely to have much of a fit when at least nine of his cards are already known to be in the minors.

(16) **Bid 3 Notrump.** Natural, balanced slam try — showing approximately a good 13 to a poor 15 HCP.

(17) **Bid 2 Spades.** Fourth suit, planning to sign off — but where? Anything could be right and you're only guessing. With honors in both of partner's suits, it is more likely to be right to play in clubs than hearts.

(18) **Bid 2 Spades.** Fourth suit, ostensibly the start of a signoff. However, when you follow with three spades on the next round, opener will know that you aren't trying to get out. (See 15.) He will place you with a game-forcing hand and at least six hearts and five spades.

The auction has been:

Opener	Responder
1 ♣	1 ♠
2 ♡	2 NT
?	

What should opener bid now?

(19) ♠ K Q 8   ♡ A 8 6 2   ◇ A   ♣ A Q 10 7 6

(20) ♠ —   ♡ K Q J 5   ◇ A K 7 3   ♣ K Q J 9 6

(21) ♠ 2   ♡ K Q 8 3   ◇ A J   ♣ A Q 10 7 6 3

(22) ♠ A Q J   ♡ A Q 10 4   ◇ —   ♣ A K J 10 9 8

(23) ♠ K J 7   ♡ A Q 10 7   ◇ Q   ♣ A J 10 6 5

(24) ♠ 6   ♡ A J 9 5   ◇ A Q   ♣ K Q J 10 9 4

(25) ♠ A   ♡ A Q 10 7 6   ◇ 3   ♣ A Q 10 8 5 4

Answers

(19) **Bid 3 Spades.** This hand is a little too good to sign off in three clubs — you may still have a spade game. Responder will be encouraged to bid it if he has anything that looks at all useful, and he can always retreat to four clubs if he has four bad spades.

(20) **Bid 3 Diamonds.** Your failure to rebid three clubs tells partner that you are still interested in game. Three diamonds describes a powerful three-suiter.

(21) **Bid 3 Clubs.** Partner wants to sign off. You have no reason to disagree with his opinion.

(22) **Bid 4 Spades.** Much too strong even for three spades which responder could pass. If he holds only four low spades, he can correct to five clubs knowing that you have a real club suit.

(23) **Bid 3 Clubs.** Not good enough for three spades. If responder passes you have not missed a game.

(24) **Bid 3 Notrump.** With all suits well stopped and a super source of tricks, your chances for game are excellent despite your having only 17 HCP.

(25) **Bid 3 Hearts.** With so much playing strength, overrule partner and make a game try, while showing at least five hearts.

After the following start:

Opener	Responder
1 ♣	1 ♠
2 ◇	2 ♡
?	

What rebid do you make as opener with:

(26) ♠ J   ♡ K Q 10   ◇ A 10 9 3   ♣ A K J 10 4

(27) ♠ Q J   ♡ K J   ◇ K Q J 7   ♣ K Q J 10 8

(28) ♠ 7   ♡ A   ◇ A K 10 9 2   ♣ A 10 9 7 3 2

Answers

(26) **Bid 2 Notrump.** Two hearts asks you to rebid three clubs, but you still want to make a game try. If responder rebids three clubs, three diamonds, or three spades over your two notrump, pass — he still wants to stop.

(27) **Bid 3 Clubs.** You have more high-card points than you did in the preceding problem, but with only one heart stopper and no aces, you won't make three notrump — so don't make a try.

(28) **Bid 3 Clubs.** If responder passes you probably do not have a game. However, if he should sign off in three diamonds he probably has four-card diamond support, so you will change your mind and raise — a nine-card diamond fit makes your hand almost worth a jump to game. This may seem inconsistent, but remember that responder may be 2-1 in the minors when he passes three clubs. He will rarely correct to three diamonds with fewer than four diamonds since he knows that opener may be 4-5 or 4-6 in the minors.

PART IV

OTHER LEBENSOHL APPLICATIONS

Chapter 11

THE LATEST WORD IN LEBENSOHL

In the preceding chapters we've studied the three basic and most widely used applications of Lebensohl:

- Lebensohl after one notrump interference
- Lebensohl after opponents' weak two-bids
- Lebensohl after opener's reverse

For most partnerships these treatments will be more than adequate to improve bidding accuracy.

We've come a long way since George Boehm published his "Lebensohl" in *The Bridge World,* with the convention's use limited to the handling of one notrump interference. Lebensohl's assimilation into expert bidding methods has been so thorough that some pairs have a dozen or more different circumstances in which they put it to use.

Let's look at a couple not previously mentioned:

Lebensohl When Our Auction Starts at the Two-Level

Consider the following auction:

RHO	You	LHO	Partner
1 ♠	Pass	2 ♠	Double
Pass	?		

What would you bid with:

(a) ♠ 6 3 2   ♡ 9 7   ◇ 10 8 3   ♣ 10 7 6 5 3

(b) ♠ 10 5 4   ♡ K 8   ◇ 10 9 4   ♣ K Q 10 8 7

If these problems seem familiar, it's because they are the same ones you faced in an earlier chapter after the auction:

LHO	Partner	RHO	You
2 ♠	Double	Pass	?

In essence, there is really no difference between these two auctions insofar as your partnership bidding is concerned. In both cases partner has made a takeout double of two spades. And in both cases you must make a three club bid, but the two hands differ widely in strength. The solution to your problem after the weak two-bid was to sign off with a Lebensohl two notrump relay to three clubs when you held hand (a), and to bid a direct forcing three clubs with hand (b).

As you have no doubt realized for yourself, there is no reason why you can't use exactly the same methods to solve problems in responding to a takeout double at the two-level. All you give up is the relatively infrequent natural two notrump response to partner's takeout double. This is a small price to pay.

Using the methods outlined above, try these bidding problems.

LHO	You	LHO	Partner
1 ♡	Pass	2 ♡	Double
Pass	?		

(1) ♠ Q 10 5 2   ♡ J 5 3 2   ◇ 8 6 5   ♣ 10 7

(2) ♠ K 5 4   ♡ 10 9 4   ◇ Q 9 8 6 5   ♣ 6 3

(3) ♠ K Q   ♡ K 6 5   ◇ 6 5 2   ♣ Q 10 8 7 2

(4) ♠ J 10   ♡ Q 10 9 5   ◇ A Q 9 5 2   ♣ Q J

(1) **Bid 2 Spades.** No Lebensohl since your suit can be bid on the same level.

(2) **Bid 2 Notrump.** Follow with three diamonds to show weakness.

(3) **Bid 3 Clubs.** The direct three-level bid shows moderate strength.

(4) **Bid 2 Notrump.** Lebensohl. Follow with three notrump, natural, showing a heart stopper and game values. A direct jump to three notrump would be stronger (unless you use "fast arrival").

Lebensohl After a One Notrump Overcall

Suppose you hold in fourth seat:

♠ K 6   ♡ 6 4   ◇ 10 7 6 4 3 2   ♣ 9 8 5 4

and hear the auction proceed:

LHO	Partner	RHO	You
1 ♡	1 NT*	Pass	?

*16-18 HCP

You probably already have a way to play in diamonds — either by bidding two diamonds to play, or by transferring to diamonds if you use transfers after notrump overcalls. (If you don't have some agreement, you should. I suggest two clubs for Stayman and Jacoby transfers in four suits, just as we discussed earlier after natural two notrump overcalls.)

But, what do you do when RHO raises hearts and takes away your transfer to diamonds?

LHO	Partner	RHO	You
1 ♡	1 NT	2 ♡	?

This puts you in the same position you were in after:

Partner	RHO	You
1 NT	2 ♡	?

And the solution is (of course you know by now) Lebensohl — exactly the same as if partner had opened one notrump rather than overcalled:

- Double is for penalties.
- Two-level bids are to play.
- Three-level bids are forcing.
- Two notrump relays to three clubs for signoff.
- Cue-bids are Stayman.
- FADS or FASS (as you wish).

Of course, your RHO is not always so cooperative. Suppose he bids something else instead of raising his partner's suit:

LHO	Partner	RHO	You
1 ♡	1 NT	2 ♠	?

Now what? Does this change things? Only slightly. There is no reason not to use Lebensohl principles here as well. The only difference between auctions (4) and (2) is that you now have two cue-bids available instead of one. How you choose to differentiate between them is a matter of personal choice. You could, for example, play that the higher cue-bid is game-forcing, while the cheaper is merely invitational. Or, you may consider playing that a "cue-bid" of your LHO's suit is not a cue-bid at all, but instead, a natural attempt to play in this suit. (In view of partner's overcall of one notrump, it is not unlikely that opener's suit, especially if it is a minor, is really your side's best trump suit.)

Using Lebensohl, how would you handle these hands?

LHO	Partner	RHO	You
1 ♠	1 NT	2 ♠	?

(1) ♠ 7 3   ♡ 9   ◇ Q 10 8 6   ♣ A K J 9 8 4

(2) ♠ 8   ♡ Q J 10 6 5 3   ◇ 9 8 5   ♣ 5 3 2

(3) ♠ 9 4   ♡ K Q 8 7   ◇ A J 8   ♣ J 9 5 3

(4) ♠ A 9 8   ♡ 5   ◇ A 10 9 3   ♣ 7 6 4 3 2

(1) **Bid 3 Clubs.** Natural and forcing.

(2) **Bid 2 Notrump.** Lebensohl. Follow with three hearts, signoff.

(3) **Bid 3 Spades.** Stayman (without a heart stopper, FADS).

(4) **Double.** Penalty.

Other Lebensohl Applications

The examples above are only a small sample of what has been done with Lebensohl in recent years. For example, it is possible to use Lebensohl after:

(1) Opener's strong jump shift to two hearts or two spades:

Opener	Responder		Opener	Responder
1 ◇	1 ♡	or	1 ♣	1 ◇
2 ♠			2 ♡	

A two notrump rebid by responder in these auctions would be Lebensohl, requesting partner to rebid three clubs. Responder can now describe his hand by rebidding his long suit or by supporting one of opener's suits; opener is warned that partner has a weak hand. (If opener has game-going values opposite an absolute minimum, he should ignore the request to bid three clubs.)

This also conserves bidding space when responder wishes to explore further, either for the "right" game or slam, since any bid by responder, other than two notrump, is constructive and forcing to game.

(2) Opener's reverse after one notrump response:

Opener	Responder		Opener	Responder
1 ◇	1 NT	or	1 ♡	1 NT
2 ♡			2 ♠	

Once again a two notrump rebid by responder can be used to describe a weak hand. Opener is asked to bid three clubs; responder then places the contract.

(3) A repeated takeout double:

LHO	Partner	RHO	Responder
1 ♠	Dbl	2 ♠	Pass
Pass	Dbl	Pass	

Lebensohl can be used in this sequence — two notrump by responder shows a weak hand and asks doubler to bid three clubs, after which responder shows his suit. All other bids by responder promise some strength.

Other possibilities for the application of the Lebensohl principle are many and varied. Virtually any auction where you would like to sign off at the three-level is a candidate for Lebensohl, just as long as an artificial two notrump bid is available.

In any case, whether your partnership adopts only basic Lebensohl over the opponents' interference with your one notrump openings or goes all out, utilizing Lebensohl in every conceivable circumstance, you are certain to be rewarded with better scores if you use this convention, plus fewer agonizing moments waiting for partner to PASS your signoffs or BID AGAIN after your forcing bids!

POST MORTEM

When used effectively, Lebensohl can be one of the most profitable weapons in your bidding arsenal. As Parts I through IV of this book illustrate, it can be employed in a wide variety of situations to distinguish good responding hands from poor ones. It can clarify which rebids are forcing, which are non-forcing, and which are simply invitational. By eliminating partnership misunderstandings, Lebensohl should add to your enjoyment of the game and improve your results. Despite the conventional agreements Lebensohl requires of your partnership, it is designed to simplify, not complicate your bidding.

Remember, Lebensohl applications do not depend upon the range of your one notrump openings and overcalls, nor on the systemic approach used by your partnership. Your bidding accuracy can be improved whether you are using Precision, Standard, Two-over-one Game-Forcing, Acol, Kaplan-Sheinwold, Weak Notrump, Strong Notrump or Intermediate Notrump simply by incorporating Lebensohl into your bidding methods.

One word of caution is necessary. As with any other convention, you and your partner must both have a clear understanding of your agreements and remember them at the table. Without clear agreements this weapon can backfire, resulting in the recording of unwanted cylinders (i.e., bulletholes) on your line on the recap sheet at match-points, and double digit losses at IMPs.

THE AUTHOR

RON ANDERSEN is one of the most successful players in the history of tournament bridge in North America. He has won innumerable National and Regional Championships and has represented the United States in several World Championships. He was the first player in ACBL history to win over 2000 master points in one year and is the only active player to capture the Barry Crane Top 500 trophy four times.

He has written ten books, dozens of pamphlets and hundreds of articles about various aspects of bridge.

50 HIGHLY-RECOMMENDED TITLES

**CALL TOLL FREE 1-800-274-2221
IN THE U.S. & CANADA TO ORDER ANY OF
THEM OR TO REQUEST OUR
FULL-COLOR 64 PAGE CATALOG OF
ALL BRIDGE BOOKS IN PRINT,
SUPPLIES AND GIFTS.**

FOR BEGINNERS
#0300 Future Champions' Bridge Series	9.95
#2130 Kantar-Introduction to Declarer's Play	7.00
#2135 Kantar-Introduction to Defender's Play	7.00
#0101 Stewart-Baron-The Bridge Book 1	9.95
#1101 Silverman-Elementary Bridge Five Card Major Student Text	4.95
#0660 Penick-Beginning Bridge Complete	9.95
#0661 Penick-Beginning Bridge Quizzes	6.95
#3230 Lampert-Fun Way to Serious Bridge	10.00

FOR ADVANCED PLAYERS
#2250 Reese-Master Play	5.95
#1420 Klinger-Modern Losing Trick Count	13.95
#2240 Love-Bridge Squeezes Complete	5.95
#0103 Stewart-Baron-The Bridge Book 3	9.95
#0740 Woolsey-Matchpoints	14.95
#0741 Woolsey-Partnership Defense	12.95
#1702 Bergen-Competitive Auctions	9.95
#0636 Lawrence-Falsecards	9.95

BIDDING — 2 OVER 1 GAME FORCE
#4750 Bruno & Hardy-Two-Over-One Game Force: An Introduction	9.95
#1750 Hardy-Two-Over-One Game Force	14.95
#1790 Lawrence-Workbook on the Two Over One System	11.95
#4525 Lawrence-Bidding Quizzes Book 1	13.95

Prices subject to change without notice.

DEFENSE
#0520 Blackwood-Complete Book of Opening Leads 17.95
#3030 Ewen-Opening Leads 15.95
#0104 Stewart-Baron-The Bridge Book 4 .... 7.95
#0631 Lawrence-Dynamic Defense 11.95
#1200 Woolsey-Modern Defensive Signalling 4.95

FOR INTERMEDIATE PLAYERS
#2120 Kantar-Complete Defensive Bridge 20.00
#3015 Root-Commonsense Bidding 15.00
#0630 Lawrence-Card Combinations 12.95
#0102 Stewart-Baron-The Bridge Book 2 .... 9.95
#1102 Silverman-Intermediate Bridge Five
      Card Major Student Text 4.95
#0575 Lampert-The Fun Way to Advanced Bridge 11.95
#0633 Lawrence-How to Read Your Opponents' Cards 9.95
#3672 Truscott-Bid Better, Play Better 11.00
#1765 Lawrence-Judgment at Bridge 9.95

PLAY OF THE HAND
#2150 Kantar-Test your Bridge Play, Vol. 1 .... 10.00
#3675 Watson-Watson's Classic Book on
      the Play of the Hand 12.00
#1932 Mollo-Gardener-Card Play Technique 12.95
#3009 Root-How to Play a Bridge Hand 12.00
#1104 Silverman-Play of the Hand as
      Declarer and Defender 4.95
#2175 Truscott-Winning Declarer Play 10.00
#3803 Sydnor-Bridge Made Easy Book 3 .... 6.00

CONVENTIONS
#2115 Kantar-Bridge Conventions 10.00
#0610 Kearse-Bridge Conventions Complete 29.95
#3011 Root-Pavlicek-Modern Bridge Conventions 15.00
#0240 Championship Bridge Series (All 36) 25.95

DUPLICATE STRATEGY
#1600 Klinger-50 Winning Duplicate Tips 12.95
#2260 Sheinwold-Duplicate Bridge 3.95

FOR ALL PLAYERS
#3889 Darvas & de V. Hart-Right Through The Pack 14.95
#0790 Simon: Why You Lose at Bridge 11.95
#4850 Encyclopedia of Bridge, Official (ACBL) 39.95

DEVYN PRESS INC.

3600 Chamberlain Lane, Suite 230, Louisville, KY 40241

1-800-274-2221

CALL TOLL FREE IN THE U.S. & CANADA TO ORDER OR TO REQUEST
OUR 64 PAGE FULL COLOR CATALOG OF BRIDGE BOOKS,
SUPPLIES AND GIFTS.

Andersen THE LEBENSOHL CONVENTION COMPLETE .... $ 6.95
Baron THE BRIDGE PLAYER'S DICTIONARY $19.95
Bergen BETTER BIDDING WITH BERGEN,
    Vol. I, Uncontested Auctions $11.95
Bergen BETTER BIDDING WITH BERGEN,
    Vol. II, Competitive Auctions .... $ 9.95
Blackwood COMPLETE BOOK OF OPENING LEADS $17.95
Boeder THINKING ABOUT IMPS $12.95
Bruno-Hardy 2 OVER 1 GAME FORCE: AN INTRODUCTION .... $ 9.95
Darvas & De V. Hart RIGHT THROUGH THE PACK $14.95
Groner DUPLICATE BRIDGE DIRECTION $14.95
Hardy
    TWO-OVER-ONE GAME FORCE $14.95
    TWO-OVER-ONE GAME FORCE QUIZ BOOK $11.95
Harris BRIDGE DIRECTOR'S COMPANION (3rd Edition) $19.95
Kay COMPLETE BOOK OF DUPLICATE BRIDGE $14.95
Kearse BRIDGE CONVENTIONS COMPLETE $29.95
Kelsey THE TRICKY GAME $11.95
Lampert THE FUN WAY TO ADVANCED BRIDGE $11.95
Lawrence
    CARD COMBINATIONS $12.95
    COMPLETE BOOK ON BALANCING $11.95
    COMPLETE BOOK ON OVERCALLS $11.95
    DYNAMIC DEFENSE $11.95
    FALSECARDS .... $ 9.95
    HAND EVALUATION $11.95
    HOW TO READ YOUR OPPONENTS' CARDS .... $ 9.95
    JUDGMENT AT BRIDGE .... $ 9.95
    PARTNERSHIP UNDERSTANDINGS .... $ 4.95
    PLAY BRIDGE WITH MIKE LAWRENCE $11.95
    PLAY SWISS TEAMS WITH MIKE LAWRENCE .... $ 7.95
    WORKBOOK ON THE TWO OVER ONE SYSTEM $11.95
Lawrence & Hanson WINNING BRIDGE INTANGIBLES .... $ 4.95
Lipkin INVITATION TO ANNIHILATION .... $ 8.95
Michaels & Cohen 4-3-2-1 MANUAL .... $ 2.95
Penick BEGINNING BRIDGE COMPLETE .... $ 9.95
Penick BEGINNING BRIDGE QUIZZES .... $ 6.95
Reese & Hoffman PLAY IT AGAIN, SAM .... $ 7.95
Rosenkranz
    BRIDGE: THE BIDDER'S GAME $12.95
    TIPS FOR TOPS .... $ 9.95
    MORE TIPS FOR TOPS .... $ 9.95
    TRUMP LEADS .... $ 7.95
    OUR MAN GODFREY $10.95
Rosenkranz & Alder BID TO WIN, PLAY FOR PLEASURE $11.95
Rosenkranz & Truscott BIDDING ON TARGET $10.95
Simon
    CUT FOR PARTNERS $9.95
    WHY YOU LOSE AT BRIDGE $11.95
Stewart & Baron
    THE BRIDGE BOOK, Vol. 1, Beginning .... $ 9.95
    THE BRIDGE BOOK, Vol. 2, Intermediate .... $ 9.95
    THE BRIDGE BOOK, Vol. 3, Advanced .... $ 9.95
    THE BRIDGE BOOK, Vol. 4, Defense .... $ 7.95
Thomas SHERLOCK HOLMES, BRIDGE DETECTIVE .... $ 9.95
Woolsey
    MATCHPOINTS $14.95
    MODERN DEFENSIVE SIGNALLING .... $ 4.95
    PARTNERSHIP DEFENSE .... $ 9.95
World Bridge Federation APPEALS COMMITTEE DECISIONS
    from the 1994 NEC WORLD CHAMPIONSHIPS .... $ 9.95